Sheffield's date with Hitler

By Neil Anderson

Copyright 2010 ACM Retro Ltd

ISBN: 978-0-9563649-3-7

All rights reserved. No part of this book may be reproduced in any form or by any electronic or mechanical means, including information storage or retrieval systems, without permission in writing from the publisher, except by a reviewer who may quote brief passages.
Every effort has been made to trace the copyright holders of photographs in this book but one or two were unreachable. We would be grateful if the photographers concerned would contact us.

Published by ACM Retro Ltd,
The Grange,
Church Street,
Dronfield,
Sheffield S18 1QB.

Visit ACM Retro at:
www.acmretro.com
Published by ACM Retro 2010.
Neil Anderson asserts the moral right to be identified as
the author of this work.
A catalogue record for this book is available from the British Library.

★ACM ЯETRO

Sheffield's date with Hitler

By Neil Anderson

Looking up High Street after the Sheffield Blitz

CONTENTS

INTRODUCTION P7

CHAPTER 1 .... P15
Sheffield's first air raid – September 1916

CHAPTER 2 .... P20
Life in 1930s Sheffield

CHAPTER 3 .... P32
The countdown to World War 2

CHAPTER 4 .... P37
Walking back from Leicester -
Sheffield city prepares for the worst...

CHAPTER 5 .... P41
"It's an air raid – not a damn jumble sale"
– life in the Anderson Shelter

CHAPTER 6 .... P47
The munitions industry and
Sheffield's Women Of Steel

CHAPTER 7 .... P53
The Sheffield Blitz –
the city's worst fears come true

CHAPTER 8 .... P67
The myths surrounding
the Sheffield Blitz

CHAPTER 9 .... P73
Direct hit on the Marples Hotel

CHAPTER 10 .... P79
December 25, 1940 – the darkest
Christmas in living memory

CHAPTER 11 .... P85
The Blitz clean up and the
Atkinsons story

CHAPTER 12 .... P91
VE Day – peace finally returns to
the streets of Sheffield

CHAPTER 13 .... P97
What's to see of the Blitz
in the 21st century

Bibliography P103

6 — Sheffield's date with Hitler

Adolf Hitler – the man who failed to break the spirit of Sheffield despite his devastating attacks

INTRODUCTION

It's hard to comprehend the true magnitude of the blitzkrieg unleashed on the City of Sheffield by Hitler's Luftwaffe on two clear, cold winter nights just a few days before Christmas in December 1940.

Even speaking first-hand to scores of people that suffered the living hell that started in the wake of the sirens that roared into life on the stroke of 7pm on Thursday, December 12; watching cinefootage of a city centre turned into a raging inferno and reading anything and everything that has ever been written about the Sheffield Blitz brings you no nearer to truly appreciating what the city and its population endured 70 years ago.

It's not as if Sheffield – and all of the UK for that matter – hadn't been through enough:

> **"I remember his horror that another generation was set to endure another world war so soon after the last."**

Steel City was still living under the dark shadow of the annihilation of its proud 'Sheffield City Battalion' that had answered Kitchener's call for men in 1914 and turned up at the Town Hall eager to do their bit for King and Country in World War One (WW1).

Their slaughter at the Battle of the Somme in the summer of 1916 is testament enough to the madness of war.

Just days later the war came to the streets of Sheffield in the shape of a devastating Zeppelin raid.

Then, just 21 years after Germany surrendered in 1918, the world was once again on the brink of global conflict in the shape of World War Two (WW2).

Totley resident Dorothy Welsby said: "I vividly remember the increasing trepidation in the 1930s as Hitler rose to power and Germany re-armed.

"My dad, Harold Hickson, was one of only a tiny number of survivors from the Sheffield City Battalion. He rarely spoke about what he'd been through in those awful months in France and I remember his horror that another generation was set to endure another world war so soon after the last."

Being lucky enough to live through nothing but peacetime makes the wanton decimation of your home city at the hands of the German Luftwaffe seem even more incredulous.

It's hard to envisage how our generation – one that struggles to cope if the bus turns up late – would adapt to the infrastructure of an entire city totally destroyed in the blink of an eye.

The Sheffield generation of 1940 did.

They did it without question.

They made incredible sacrifices; the Government's 'Keep Calm and Carry On' message could have been written about the city in the aftermath of the Sheffield Blitz.

Dorothy Welsby (right) with her father Harold Hickson (middle) and mother Mabel Treece Hickson

8 · Sheffield's date with Hitler

Looking up a busy Haymarket towards Fitzalan Square prior to the Sheffield Blitz

Sheffield's date with Hitler

Members of Sheffield City Battalion at their camp at Redmires, on the outskirts of Sheffield, November 1914, prior to their Somme offensive - Harold Hickson, top row, third from right. Harold revisited the photo after the Somme offensive and wrote a poignant 'K' to signify those killed and 'W' for the wounded

Their steadfast response was held up as a blueprint for others to follow.

The fact Sheffield was so high on Hitler's hit list came as no real surprise to the people of the city at the time – its heavy industry was the backbone of the country's war effort and it was always going to be a target.

Many expected the attack far earlier.

Thankfully, as the Sheffield Blitz didn't happen until 15 months into the war, the city had come a long way in preparation for the worst: public air raid shelters were widespread and Anderson Shelters constructed.

The decimation of much of the city centre is well documented together with the Luftwaffe's large scale failure to wipe out the East End and its heavy industry.

But what is often forgotten is the devastation across the rest of Sheffield.

From Woodseats to Wisewood; Manor to Meersbrook; Ranmoor to Rivelin; Wybourn to Walkley the bombers laid waste to an entire city over two nights just a few days before Christmas 1940.

Prosperous residential streets and thoroughfares of today like: Westbourne Road, Abbeydale Road South, Cobnar Road in Woodseats, Bocking Lane in Beauchief and Hawksley Avenue in Hillsborough – they were all badly hit alongside scores of others.

The death and destruction was on a truly unimaginable scale and many bombsites were left derelict for years to come.

Massive city centre shopping institutions like Atkinsons, Cockaynes, Redgates and C&A Modes, along with their glittering Christmas displays, were razed to the ground in the blink of an eye.

In short, the two night raids made a staggering 40,000 people homeless; killed or injured 2,160 people and damaged 78,000 homes across the city.

There's a communal grave for 134 of the victims in Sheffield's City Road Cemetery.

Harold Hickson – one of the few Sheffield City Battalion survivors from the disastrous Somme offensive in WW1

Sheffield in the 1930s

Sheffield's date with Hitler

A royal visit to see the devastation in Sheffield after the Blitz

Extraordinary events led to extraordinary actions by individuals and incredible acts of heroism were reported, leading to George Medals for six citizens of Sheffield.

King George VI and Queen Elizabeth toured the city in the wake of the devastating raids to boost morale and inspect the damage.

For decades it has been assumed that the East End and its heavy industry was Hitler's main target, but this book raises serious doubts about whether that was ever the case

Prime Minister Winston Churchill followed close behind; speaking through loudspeakers to a 20,000 crowd in the city centre and giving his trademark 'V' for 'Victory' sign to rapturous applause.

Seventy years on from the Sheffield Blitz there's not that much left to see of the devastation.

The odd unexploded bomb is still discovered – there was one found only a few years ago following excavation works in The Wicker area – but other than that everywhere has been rebuilt.

But there are a few, tell tale signs and well hidden clues as to what happened in two of the darkest days in Sheffield's history if you look closely.

Check the pillars at the front of Sheffield City Hall – you can still see the marks where they were hit by flying shrapnel.

Other than that, the building was largely untouched and actually became a feeding station for the homeless in the aftermath of the attacks.

Wander down city centre shopping thoroughfare, The Moor, and try and find a building that pre-dates 1950 – you won't find a thing, the whole area was completed wiped out and subsequently rebuilt.

The same can be said for much of High Street, King Street, Angel Street and other great swathes of the heart of the city centre as it was in 1940.

For decades it has been assumed that the East End and its heavy industry was Hitler's main target but this book raises serious doubts about whether that was ever the case.

Recently uncovered German bombing maps of Sheffield highlight the densely populated suburbs, hospitals, universities as the prime targets.

If that was indeed the case then the raids were far more successful than once thought.

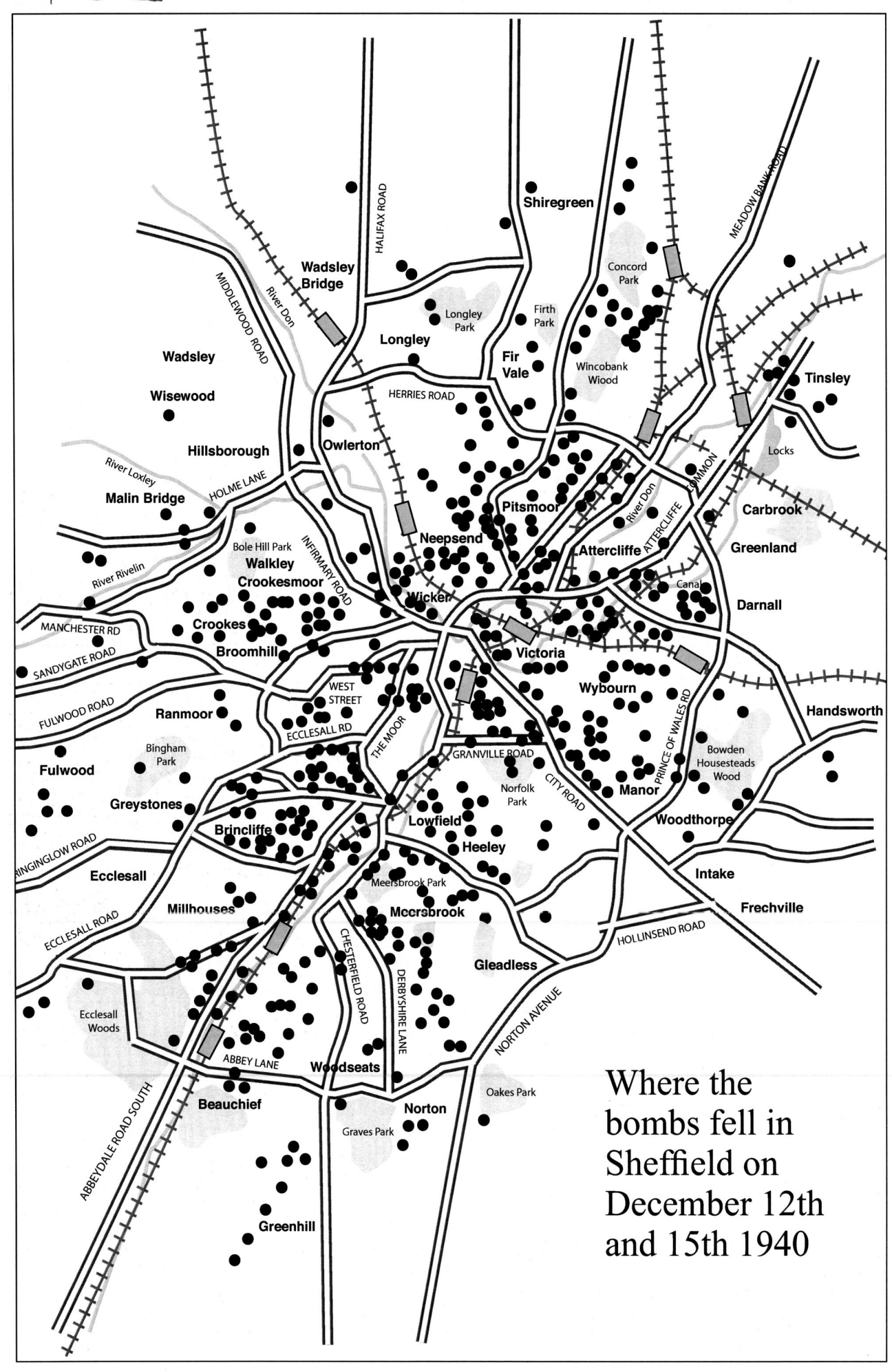

12 **Sheffield's date with Hitler**

Where the bombs fell in Sheffield on December 12th and 15th 1940

Sheffield's date with Hitler

Keep calm and carry on – defiance in the face of Southey Hill parachute mine damage

Fargate on VE Day

14 — Sheffield's date with Hitler

Daddy, what did YOU do in the Great War?

A popular recruitment tactic in WW1 was posters designed to shame men into enlistment – the slaughter of the Sheffield City Battalion didn't exactly have potential new conscripts beating a path to the Town Hall to sign up, so new and more devious measures were needed. Poster designer Savile Lumley refused to be associated with it at the time due to its emotionally manipulative tactic.

CHAPTER ONE
Sheffield's first air raid - September 1916

It's impossible to imagine the sheer terror faced by any Sheffielder that heard the menacing drone overhead that fateful night in September, 1916.

They'd have opened the curtains to see the vast, German Zeppelin L-22 airship in the cloudy sky over the city, about to unleash living hell on a previously unimaginable scale.

It was just before 10pm when people living beyond the city's southern boundaries first spotted the huge airship cruising menacingly towards Sheffield.

It is believed it followed the brightly shining railway lines as they weaved their way from the south of the region to reach the city.

Sheffield was thought to be beyond the range of German aeroplanes at that point in aviation history – Zeppelins, as its population was about to discover, were a different matter.

The Zeppelin started off by circling clockwise over the city to help get its bearings

Only a few months earlier it had been unthinkable for a civilian population sited hundreds of miles away from a battlefront to be in any danger whatsoever.

But now, barely a decade after the Wright Brothers had pioneered the world's first powered flight, the Kaiser had changed the nature of conflict forever with the start of Zeppelin raids on the UK's towns and cities and, in doing so, brought the whole nation to the front line of battle.

Little has been written about Sheffield's first air raid. Maybe the situation suited some who would rather have forgotten the city's preparation – or total lack of it - that night.

Sheffield learned a tragic lesson in the importance of air raid planning and readiness the night the 585 foot long machine sidled menacingly into town at a top speed of 60mph; almost unnoticed by the local anti-aircraft defence officers who were busy lording it up at a social function taking place at Leopold Street's Grand Hotel.

> **Fliege nach England,**
> **England wird abgebrannt.**
> **Fly to England,**
> **England shall be burned down.**
> German children's song.

The defences were described as a "fiasco" and "shambolic" in the aftermath of the attack on the evening of September 25/26, 1916, that left 28 people killed and many more injured.

Sheffield's strategic importance as a vast munitions supplier to the country's war effort was well known by the Germans and the city was always going to be a target.

But factories were largely missed and it was workers' homes nearby that bore the brunt of the city's first air raid.

Kapitanleutnant Martin Dietrich made his approach to Sheffield from the south-eastern corner of the city. It was around 12.20am when the L-22 finally arrived overhead.

The Zeppelin started off by circling clockwise over the city to help get its bearings before dropping wave after wave of incendiaries and high explosives over the suburbs of Pitsmoor and Attercliffe.

The first bomb hit Burngreave Cemetery. The deafening explosion destroyed a boundary wall, closely followed by the second bomb which fell close to Danville Street where the first fatality of the night occurred.

Two elderly women living in a house off Grimethorpe Road were the next two names to be added to the grim roll call.

Shrapnel from a blast killed the next victim – a man believed to be 59 year old Thomas Wilson who was looking out of a window at 73 Petre Street after chatting with neighbours minutes earlier.

He was almost decapitated by flying shrapnel.

A 57-year-old woman who lived at 43 Writtle Street was next to lose her life through massive wounds and shock.

Kapitanleutant Martin Dietrich, the man who commanded the Zeppelin L22 that hit Sheffield in September, 1916

16 | Sheffield's date with Hitler

Sheffield women were recruited to the city's munitions factories in WW1 as the menfolk went to war

Sheffield's date with Hitler

Sheffield Daily Independent's reporting of the coroner's inquest into the devastating attack that appeared on Friday, September 29, 1916, sounds shocking in the graphic detail it gives, compared to the way it would be presented today.
It also rightly questions the lack of warning. Wartime reporting restrictions forbade the paper from naming Sheffield – it is instead referred to as a 'Midland town':

"Tragic and pathetic details were related to a Coroner of a Midlands town, who opened an inquest yesterday upon victims of the Zeppelin raid of the night of 26 September. The victims were eight men, 10 women and 10 children.
"The Coroner said the jury would hear some pathetic evidence in one case of a father, mother, and five children, all cut off together, and other cases of perhaps lesser degree of poignant grief. Whatever the circumstances might be, their sympathies went out to the sorrowing relatives."
The report goes on to list the deaths one by one.

"The first case taken was that of a woman aged 36 years, wife of a labourer. Her husband said he hurried to the attic to fetch his children and take them into the cellar, and shouted to his wife to follow. As he reached the cellar there was an explosion. His wife exclaimed, "Oh Bill my leg's off". She died three hours afterwards.

"Concerning a labourer and his wife and five children aged 14, 11, 8, 5 and 2, it was stated that their house was completely destroyed by a bomb, and when they were taken from the ruins all but the 14-year-old boy were dead. He was extensively bruised about the face and head and there were contusions all over his body. Death took place a few hours later from shock and the injuries.

"An elderly married woman got out of bed when the first bomb dropped and was passing across the room to get her child when a bomb struck her in the back, tearing it open. Her body was nearly severed at the trunk. She died in hospital. [The elderly married woman, we now know, was Elizabeth Bellamy of 43 Writtle Street.]

"A youth, with his arm in a sling, described the death of his father with whom he was sleeping. Witness was awakened by the explosion of a bomb and he heard his father groaning. His mother shouted but received no reply from his father so he jumped out of bed and shook him, but could get no answer. Another bomb then struck the witness on the finger and something hit him on the head and he was knocked senseless.

"In the case of an elderly man it was stated that he went to the window when the first bomb dropped, but the remainder of the occupants of the house went under the stairs. A little grandchild went to fetch him away from the window but as she spoke to him a bright light appeared and she saw no more of him.

"A young married couple and their baby, aged 14 months, were in bed when their house was struck by a bomb and completely wrecked. All three were killed.

"In the case of a 28-year-old woman and her two daughters, aged 6 and 4, it was stated that their bodies were dug out of the cellar of the house which was wrecked.

"When the body of a 59-year-old married man was extricated from the ruins of his house, he was found to have a pipe of tobacco in one hand and a box of matches in the other, apparently having been about to light up. His wife, and daughters, aged twelve, were also killed, and another married couple living next door were found dead with them, having joined with them when the raid commenced.

"The opinion was expressed by a relative of a young married couple, one of whom was found in the road and the other in the backyard, that they had been blown out of the house by the explosion of the bomb, for it appeared they had been in bed at the time.

"Screams were heard to come from two women who lived together, and immediately afterwards, the house collapsed, and both were found dead.

"An 11-year-old boy was killed by the collapse of the house just as his mother was fetching him from bed.

"A 32-year-old man had just been with three others to tell someone to extinguish a light when the first bomb exploded. He was found shortly afterwards within three yards of the bomb hole. The same bomb had blown in the side of the house, but the occupants were in the cellar, and escaped injury."

Elizabeh Bellamy - killed by a bomb

CITY OF SHEFFIELD.

PRECAUTIONS TO BE OBSERVED IN CASE OF AIR RAIDS

When reliable information is received of enemy aircraft approaching the danger zone of Sheffield, Electric Buzzers will be sounded for a period of three minutes in a series of triple blasts.

This warning should not unduly alarm the public being a precautionary measure for them to carry out the following instructions:—

When the buzzers sound—

By Day.—Persons should seek nearest available cover and refrain from congregating in streets.

By Night.—Seek cover, preferably in basement. Extinguish all (except candle) light; keep doors closed and windows darkened.

SCHOOLS.
(Day).—Children should be dispersed as quickly as possible so that they may reach their homes without delay.

(Night).—All classes to be abandoned and lights extinguished as expeditiously as possible.

PLACES OF WORSHIP.
(Day).—The congregation should disperse and proceed to their respective homes.

(Night).—The service should at once be discontinued and congregation disperse and all lights be extinguished.

PLACES OF ENTERTAINMENT, &c.
(Day).—The audience should disperse and proceed home.

(Night).—The same instruction as above to be observed and lights to be at once extinguished.

TRAMCARS.
(Day).—Drivers will proceed to the nearest Depôt.

(Night).—All lights to be switched off and car to be taken with despatch to the Depôt, conformably with Departmental instructions.

DRIVERS OF OTHER VEHICLES.
Mechanically or horse-propelled vehicles should seek cover. No lights will be permitted.

STREET LIGHTING.
All street lamps and external lights will be extinguished. On no account will bull's-eye lanterns, electric torches, etc., be permitted to be used. Striking of matches in the streets is strictly prohibited.

SHOP LIGHTS MUST BE EXTINGUISHED.
NO FURTHER WARNING WILL BE GIVEN.

"DANGER PAST" SIGNAL.
When all danger has passed, the buzzers will be sounded by a continuous blast of one minute duration.

NOTE—This method of warning will also serve the purpose of mobilizing Regular and Special Police, Volunteer Firemen, Doctors, Lamplighters, etc., for Air Raid duty.

F. A. WARLOW,
Lord Mayor.

Town Hall, Sheffield,
4th February, 1916.

WW1 air raid instructions for Sheffield citizens

Sheffield's date with Hitler

Although Sheffield had numerous air raid warnings during WW1 there was only this one actual attack.

As well as the fatalities and injuries, the raid caused serious damage to 89 houses, one hotel and a chapel. A further 150 houses were damaged to a lesser degree.

Of the 28 deaths, 19 of the victims are buried in Burngreave Cemetery, including seven from the Tyler family from Corby Street nearby.

The air raid warning, when it did finally come that night, was the 14th Sheffield had had since the outbreak of war.

Not everyone followed official advice which advised people to take refuge in their cellars. Many thought they'd be safer in Sheffield's parks, woods and open spaces.

Others had a far more gung-ho attitude and viewed the air raid warnings as a spectacle and believed the city's land-locked location together with its surrounding hills would make it impossible for a Zeppelin to find.

Attitudes changed for good after that night.

The Zeppelin's parting shots were over Darnall and Tinsley Park Colliery, dropping several more incendiary bombs, before heading out to sea and returning safely to Germany.

Although a number of anti-aircraft guns and searchlights were located around Sheffield, cloud prevented their crews from seeing the Zeppelin that night. A gun sited at Shiregreen was the only one to take action. It fired two rounds in the approximate direction of the airship without result.

The Zeppelin L22 airship that bombed Sheffield in September, 1916

Extracts from a personal letter sent just days after the raid by a Sheffield resident which demonstrates what kind of impact the attack had on ordinary people:

"Dear Aunt Ellen

"Just a line to let you know we are still living, although we thought our number was up on Monday night.

"I do not know if you have heard we had a Zeppelin Raid on Monday about midnight and we were heavily bombed.

"I shall never forget the awful sensation as long as I live. About 10.45pm the alarm buzzers went and within half an hour the streets were empty but for the patrol cars in total darkness. I think we all realised it was more serious than ever before as the soldiers, police and specials worked like Trojans, and were very alert.

"Alf had not got home. He was down at Alice's and they would not hear of him coming out when the alarm went, it was too dangerous.

"Suddenly we heard a droning sound overhead, which came stronger every minute, then there were two sounds that came from another direction and Elsie clutched hold of Harry's arm and screamed out 'they are here' – she trembled like a leaf.

"The Sheffield people kept saying they [the Zeppelin] will never get here.

"Well we got our big coats on and sat at my bedroom window and about 2 o'clock we saw a great red flare go across the sky and a second later a terrific crash. Then another. They were high explosive shells and they shook the earth. Then a number of pale green lights like lightening with terrible crashes after each one. They lit the entire sky up. They were incendiary bombs. There were 15 bombs dropped. I sat and watched it all though. I could not move. I felt numbed."

Music hall star averts Zeppelin panic

A story is told about how popular music hall star of the day, George Robey, nicknamed the 'Prime Minister of Mirth', averted widespread panic at the Sheffield Empire theatre (pictured above) that night.

A packed house was enjoying his inimitable style of entertainment via a song which he ended each verse with the rallying cry, "Aw, shurrup!" During the song, the drone of Zeppelin engines could be clearly heard overhead which sent shock waves and a gasp of panic through the audience.

Robey stopped singing, listened quizzically and then shouted in total disgust, "Aw shurrup!".

The audience burst out in laughing and the panic subsided.

The German Zeppelin raiders of WW1 were demonised as 'baby killers' for causing indiscriminate civilian casualties and mass panic.

CHAPTER TWO
Life in 1930s Sheffield

Looking up London Road

Sheffield in the thirties was definitely an era of two halves.

The early years were a period of mass unemployment and depression following the country's General Strike in 1926 and the Stock Market Crash in New York three years later.

America's economic collapse sent shockwaves across the world and the effect on the UK was devastating as the demand for the country's goods dried up almost overnight.

By the end of 1930, unemployment in the country had increased from one million to a staggering two and a half million.

Sheffield's steel and heavy industry – which was all heavily export orientated – was one of the worst hit areas.

In fact the thirties were probably the most difficult time in living memory for many in the city.

Queuing at soup kitchens, mass unemployment and families left destitute became a way of life in Northern England.

A Government report in the mid 1930s estimated that 25% of the country's population

Queuing at soup kitchens, mass unemployment and families left destitute became a way of life in Northern England

were existing on a subsistence diet; signs of child malnutrition were commonplace.

Sheffield of the time was no oil painting according to celebrated writer George Orwell.

He said: "It has a population of half a million and it contains fewer decent buildings than the average East Anglian village of five hundred".

Sheffield, he also pointed out, "could justly claim to be called the ugliest town in the Old World".

The city, like most of the UK, was far from recovered from the effects of WW1 which caused massive financial instability right across Europe.

Sheffield's date with Hitler

Looking up Surrey Street with Sheffield Town Hall on the left, in the 1930s

22 | Sheffield's date with Hitler

Inside the toy department at Empire Trading Stamp Company on Howard Street

ATKINSON'S
Great Christmas Grotto' & Toytown

Atkinson's
BY MAGIC CANNON to
FAIRY TOY TOWN
Come early.   Presents 6d.
ATKINSON'S, THE MOOR, SHEFFIELD.

Sheffield's date with Hitler

The boom period that transformed the outlook of the city in the latter half of the 1930s and signalled an end to the dole queues came with unspeakable costs.

As Hitler's inexorable rise to power continued, and Germany rearmed, so did the UK.

Sheffield's steelmills were once more at full capacity as the munitions orders rolled in.

But it certainly wasn't all doom and gloom.

One of the biggest revolutions was in Sheffield's cinemas, as talking films appeared for the first time and heralded a boom time for the silver screen.

The car was already a serious problem. In 1930 alone, 70 people were killed in serious road accidents in the city with a further 1,500 injured

It was also boom time on a truly unimaginable scale for football in the city.

In 1935, SWFC not only reached the FA Cup Final, they actually won it.

SUFC were in the final the following year – unfortunately they lost.

Spectator sport was positively booming in the city. We had a baseball team (Sheffield Dons); a national boxing champion (Johnny Cuthbert); 10,000 turned to witness the first greyhound meeting at Owlerton Stadium and Bramall Lane doubled as a cricket ground.

If we weren't watching it we were taking part – just not together...

The open air pool at Millhouses Park was a very popular venue; though men and women were not allowed to swim together.

Sunbathing with the opposite sex was also strictly off limits. There was even an iron fence to ensure this unholy alliance was kept apart (though they were allowed to chat through the railings).

Many things that are bugbears today were considered a nightmare way back then.

The car was already a serious problem. In 1930 alone, 70 people were killed in road accidents in the city with a further 1,500 injured.

Traffic congestion was considered to be a major issue and Belisha beacon pedestrian crossings made their Sheffield debut in 1934 together with 30 miles per hour speed limits.

The Wicker, the city's busiest road, was already used by an average of 11,127 motor vehicles, 7,030 cyclists, 3,279 trams and 729 horses every single day.

Above: Firs Hill School percussion band in 1930

Left: Looking towards Sheffield City Hall under construction

Sheffield's date with Hitler

The 21st century war on binge drinking would have been proud – a study reported the number of people charged with drunkenness in Sheffield, per thousand population, was the lowest in the country in 1930.

Film stars Laurel and Hardy visited the city in 1932 and made personal appearances at the Cinema House.

Sheffield might have risen to one of the UK's top clubbing destinations in the 1990s but it was already on the way in October 1932 when 'gramophone record recitalist' (the early name for a DJ) Christopher Stone spun discs for an audience of 3,000 at the city centre's Victoria Hall. We're presuming it wasn't an all-nighter.

The city centre has had some varied sights over the years but few top the marauding tiger on December 2, 1933. It was at large for a full four hours after it decided a trip round town

Sheffield City Hall under construction – it opened in 1932

The city centre has had some varied sights over the years but few top the marauding tiger on December 2, 1933. It was at large for a full four hours

was far more preferable to being locked up in a cage at the Empire Theatre sited just off The Moor.

21st century Sheffield boasts some of the fastest broadband connections in the country. We were pretty well connected even in 1934 with the city boasting 90,728 wireless licences – one for every seven of the population. Sheffield University was expanding even then – in November 1934 it was after £500,000 to fulfil its dreams.

Sheffield's date with Hitler

Looking up from Moorhead towards the site of the modern day Peace Gardens

Left: Fitzalan Square – a direct hit on the seven-storey Marples building to the left of the picture caused the biggest single human tragedy on the first night of the Sheffield Blitz

The Darnall Medical Aid parade near the Wellington Inn in the early 1930s

Sheffield's date with Hitler

Surrey Street's Central Library under construction

Lack of foresight has been blamed for many a failed Sheffield project

Lack of foresight has been blamed for many a failed Sheffield project but it definitely can't be blamed for the short-lived Sheffield Airport – Lord Mayor, Alderman P.J.M. Turner, was asking for one as far back as January 1935.

Spats between different entertainment genres became a regular issue in the 1990s for Sheffield City Hall as artists in the upstairs Oval Hall complained about noise pollution from club nights in the downstairs ballroom.

It was regularly said that the 1930s art deco building had not been geared up for the leisure needs of the late 20th century.

Unfortunately it seems it was never geared up.

Pride of Sheffield, Johnny Cuthbert (left), with ferocious looking opponent Frank McAloran – the pair slugged it out at Edmund Drill Hall in 1931 in front of 5,000

High Street's HL Brown and, to the right, Cockaynes – both stores were destroyed in the Sheffield Blitz

Sheffield's date with Hitler

In February 1938 Adolf Busch and Rudolf Serkin refused to start their Memorial Hall recital because of noise from the dance band in the ballroom.

In August 1938 Sheffield experienced its first real sign that war was on the way with its first blackout for testing air raid precautions.

War of a different kind was declared in April 1939 as pensioners marched through Sheffield on their way to a mass meeting at Burngreave to demand higher pensions – there were no records of any arrests we're glad to say.

In August 1938 Sheffield experienced its first real sign that war was on the way

Above: Looking along Pinstone Street and down towards Moorhead with St Paul's Church in the foreground that was demolished in 1938 and is these days home to the Peace Gardens

Left: A busy Fargate

COLES SALE
BEGINS TO-MORROW MORNING AT 9 A.M.

TO-MORROW—the first Shopping day of the New Year coincides with the opening of what promises to be the Greatest Bargain Event of 1930. Throughout Five Vast Floors, Stocks have been drastically reduced, providing hundreds of Sensational opportunities. A glance at the examples below will indicate the necessity of an early call.

Five Vast Floors Packed with Quality Bargains

JUMPERS & CARDIGANS

(Top). Representing a choice range of Ladies' Model Jumpers in Wool and Silk faced. A particularly wide range of colours. Actual Value 25/-.
SALE PRICE... 10/-

(Bottom). Representing a Group of Shetland Knit Cardigans in Stripe and Plain colours. Attractive Pastel and all shades.
SALE PRICE TO CLEAR... 6/11

MAC. OFFERS

Remarkable offer of a collection of slightly soiled Macs. In Rayon Silk and Indiana. All Reduced to Clear.
SALE PRICE... 10/-

Chosen from a collection of Model Jumper Suits in attractive Jacquered effect. Jumpers have plain coloured Skirts. Actual Value 94/6.
SALE PRICE 29/6

FABRICS

All Silk Crepe-de-Chine
An amazing offer that it will be impossible to repeat. This supple and bright All Silk Crepe is something truly exceptional, and an early visit is advised. Available in a large range of attractive colours. 38" wide. Actual Value 6/11.
SALE PRICE 3/11½

Rich Chiffon Velvet
500 yards of beautiful quality Rich Chiffon Velvet, with rich deep Pile. In a range of useful Evening Shades and Black. Reduced to nearly half usual price. 40" wide. Actual Value 12/11.
SALE PRICE 6/11

All Wool Crepe-de-Chine
A fashionable Dress Fabric with a most attractive Crepe effect. In Fawn, Almond, Bottle, Cocoa, Nigger, Saxe, Lido Red, Navy and Black. 54" wide. Actual Value 5/11.
SALE PRICE 3/11½

Plain & Printed Cord Velveteen
A good quality Cord Velveteen in charming Prints, also Plain. In a particularly wide range of smart Colourings. Ideal for Dresses, Dressing Gowns and Kiddies' wear. 27" wide. Actual Value 2/6.
SALE PRICE Plain 1/9½   SALE PRICE Print 1/11½
(Ground Floor)

COAT STOCKS REDUCED.

(Left). Representing a special group of smart Tweed Coats, Lined throughout Fur Fabric and handsomely trimmed to tone. Season's prices 94/6 and 5 gns.
SALE PRICE 59/6

(Centre). Representing a group of charming Tweed Coats. A variety of charming designs and colourings, handsomely trimmed and lined throughout. Season's Price 94/6.
SALE PRICE 39/6

(Right). Representing a group of Lightweight Tweed Coats, tailored, representing exceptional value. Season's Price 73/6.
SALE PRICE 19/11

EXCEPTIONAL OFFERS IN LINGERIE and CORSETS

Wonderful Offer of Ladies' Ripple Cloth Dressing Gowns. Beautifully Embroidered, they tie at the side. One pocket and made in ample proportion. Actual Value 8/11.
SALE PRICE 5/-

LOCKNIT KNICKERS
Ladies' Heavy Quality Locknit Directoire Knickers. The fabric is absolutely guaranteed. Available in colours of White, Pink, Sky, Mauve, Biska, Geranium, Nil, Apple, Peach, Champ, Puritan and Lupin. Actual Values: Women's size 8/11. Outsize 10/9.
SALE PRICE, Women's 5/6   Outsize 7/6.

SCARF WRAPS
Wonderful Offer of All Wool Canadian Scarf Wraps in White, Mauve, Pink and Sky. Actual Value 5/11.
SALE PRICE 3/3

A quantity of famous makes of Corsets, such as "Gossard," etc., have been arranged in Six Bargain Priced Groups Ranging from **8/-**

BARGAINS IN GOWNS

(On the Right). Representing a group of charming Evening Gowns in Rayon Faille Silk. Exceptional Value. Season's Price 94/6.
SALE PRICE 59/6

A Group of attractive Coat Frocks in several delightful Pastel Shades and Navy. Season's Prices 73/6, 94/6.
SALE PRICE TO CLEAR 19/11

UMBRELLAS

Special Clearance Group of Ladies' "Chubbys" with Covers. Strong and durable. Bordered. Exceptional offer.
SALE PRICE 5/11

Wonderful Offer of a Group of Ladies' attractive Frocks in Printed Cotton and Cotton Granite. Reduced to
SALE PRICE EACH 5/-

GLOVES

300 pairs of Ladies' Real Nappa Gloves, Two Dome Fastening and Fleecy lining throughout. A most useful glove at Bargain price. Available in Tan only. Actual Value 5/11.
SALE PRICE, PAIR 3/11

Below we give brief details of three outstanding values received by wire from our Glove Buyer this morning. They will be available to-morrow, of course:—

A quantity of Degrain Samples. Usually 10/11 and 12/11.
SALE PRICE, PER PAIR 5/11

Fur Top Nappa Lined Gloves. Usually 8/11.
SALE PRICE, PER PAIR 3/11

Remarkable Offer of a quantity of Lined Suede Plain Gloves. Usually 8/11.
SALE PRICE, PER PAIR 3/11

Wonderful HOSIERY Offer

1,000 pairs Ladies' "Spunsheen" Hose. Full Fashioned, with Dainty Lace Clox. A perfect fitting Hose of smart appearance. Available in Bark, Antone, Grain, Gazelle, Beechnut, New Brown, etc. Actual Value 2/11.
PER PAIR 1/6½
(Ground Floor)

HOUSEHOLD LINENS

Offer of 1,000 PILLOW CASES
1,000 Housewife Pillow Cases in Plain and Twill weave. The famous "Donna" and Horrockses make.
SALE PRICE TO CLEAR EACH 1/-
Bolster Cases to match, 20 x 40, 1/11

REMARKABLE SHEET OFFER
200 Pairs of Heavy Weight White Twill Sheets, to be cleared at the bargain prices below:—
Single Bed size, Pair **SALE PRICE 9/11**
Double Bed Size, Pair **SALE PRICE 13/11**
Large Double Bed Size **SALE PRICE 16/11**

HEMSTITCHED PILLOW CASES
595 Hemstitched Bay Pillow Cases, Housewife Style. Size 20x30 **SALE PRICE EACH 1/1½**
250 Bolster Cases to match, 2/3 each.

200 Pairs of BLANKET SHEETS
Sensational Offer of 200 pairs Fleecy Blanket Sheets. All Cream.
Size 60 x 80 **SALE PRICE PAIR 6/9**
Size 70 x 90 **SALE PRICE PAIR 7/11**

Sheffield's date with Hitler

31

Above: inside Tuckwoods Stores Ltd on Fargate

Walsh's store that was completely demolished in the Blitz

CHAPTER THREE
The countdown to World War 2

Preparing for the worst - a gas mask drill in Sheffield

The 1919 signing of The Treaty of Versailles was supposed to ensure the horrors of WW1 were never repeated. In fact it succeeded in doing the exact opposite.

Over the next two decades it helped exacerbate German grievances to become the main cause of a far bloodier and widespread global conflict, WW2.

The treaty was approved by the 32 country strong Allied Peace Congress.

Germany was forced to take full responsibility for the war and the stringent terms of the 80,000 word document virtually disarmed it.

Dishonour was the order of the day for the country on May 6, 1919, when the treaty was rubber-stamped.

Germany was forced to give up its overseas empire with the map of Europe substantially redrawn.

The country was forced to pay massive financial reparations to the Allies as well as being forced to surrender all merchant ships over 1,600 tons, a quarter of its fishing fleet, industrial machinery, railway locomotives and rolling stock, coal and much more.

The country was humiliated and nobody took it any worse than a young German army political-instruction officer named Adolf Hitler.

He was already clearly demonstrating his political tendencies within months of the war ending.

In September 1919 Hitler was ordered to investigate a small, right wing party - the German Workers' Party in Munich.

He did far more than investigate. Hitler joined it, became a regular public speaker and was its leader within two years.

His nationalistic opposition to The Treaty of Versailles was designed to have widespread appeal – his advocacy of strong-arm tactics

Sheffield's date with Hitler

German troops parade through Warsaw on October 5, 1939, after their invasion of Poland

Sheffield's date with Hitler

Right: Italian dictator Benito Mussolini with Adolf Hitler in Munich, Germany, 1940

As close to England as Adolf Hitler ever got – standing in front of the Eiffel Tower in 1940 after the fall of France

and violence to get his own way was very much in evidence from the early days.

By 1923 Germany had fallen behind in payment of reparations and France and Belgium occupied the country's main industrial region, the Ruhr, as a reprisal in an attempt to make it pay up. One of the main reasons for the country's failure to keep up with payments was the decline in the value of the German Mark, which virtually collapsed.

The financial weakness of the country only added to the growing political unrest – a situation that Hitler quickly capitalised on with his renamed National Socialist German Workers' Party (NSDAP), the organisation that became better known as the Nazi Party.

He attempted to seize power in Bavaria, in collaboration with future Nazi party mainstay General Ludendorff, a prominent military leader in WW1.

The ill-planned coup earned Hitler a spell in prison.

He ended up serving only nine months of a much longer sentence and spent his time penning the political diatribe Mein Kampf (usually translated as 'my struggle') – a collection of anti-Communist, anti-Semitic ramblings that had the intention of looking for future Lebensraum ('living space') for Germany in Eastern Europe.

His incarceration gave him the time to learn the importance of the appearance of legality – something he attempted to convey right up to the outbreak of WW2.

In June 1929 Hitler joined with the Nationalist Party to oppose a plan for the final settlement of the German reparations bill.

His campaign brought new financial backing for his Nazi Party and saw him become a national figure in Germany.

October 1929 saw the collapse of the New York Stock Exchange and the start of a devastating worldwide economic depression that only added to Germany's problems.

By September the following year, Hitler's Nazis became the second largest party in the country with 20 per cent of the vote in the German elections.

The next year the country's acute economic problems were made worse still with the collapse of German bank Darmstadter National.

In spring 1932 Hitler stood in the German presidential elections.

Unemployment now stood at a staggering six million and was rising fast – those lucky enough to have a job were likely to be low paid.

All in all it was the perfect breeding ground for the ideological, class and racial doctrines adopted by the Nazi party.

Hitler lost to Hindenburg in the election but support for him was growing by the day.

By July the Nazis had become the largest party in the Reichstag, the German parliament, after elections in which the Nazi SA, the paramilitary wing, did much to intimidate the opposition.

In January 1933 the rising tide of nationalistic support for Adolf Hitler saw him elected as chancellor of Germany.

The growing support only fueled his fanatical ambitions and ability to stop at nothing to get his own way.

The following month the Reichstag was set on fire. Fingers are pointed at Nazi involvement but four Communists are tried and executed. It all works nicely in Hitler's favour.

Intimidation campaigns against opponents on any side are stepped up by the Nazis.

By October, Hitler had ended Germany's participation in disarmament conferences.

June 1934's infamous Night of the Long Knives sees him remove key enemies from within his own party – especially the SA. At least 85 political opponents are killed – many suspect the actual number was far higher.

By August, Hitler had proclaimed himself Führer and Reich Chancellor following the death of President Hindenburg.

Sheffield's date with Hitler

German armed forces then swore allegiance to their country's new head of state.

By March 1935 Hitler had introduced compulsory military service and directly contravened The Treaty of Versailles by announcing the existence of a German air force – Britain, France and Italy condemn the breaches.

Persecution of the Jews in Germany is increased via the issue of the Nuremberg decrees.

In January 1937 Hitler formally abrogates virtually every aspect of the Treaty of Versailles, in an infamous Reichstag speech, claiming it impossible for a great power to accept such restrictions.

In November, Hitler admits he will probably need to use force to achieve his wish for Lebensraumn in Eastern Europe and is considering action against Austria and Czechoslovakia, in the short term, to achieve his ambitions.

Britain and France decide nothing should be done about any German move against Austria.

France's own treaty obligations leave no option but to side with Czechoslovakia if the worst happens there.

"You knew that something was going to happen eventually. You knew there was a war coming."

The knock-on effect would leave Britain with no alternative but to be drawn into a war in a bid to stop a French defeat.

Britain was left with little option but to try and obtain an agreement between Germany and Czechoslovakia, which meant only one thing, leaning on the Czechs to make concessions.

By March the following year, Austria had been annexed by Hitler as German troops crossed the border.

The Italian fascist leader, Benito Mussolini, once vehemently opposed to Hitler entering Austria, doesn't lift a finger.

Austria is proclaimed a province of Germany on March 13, 1938; anything left of the Treaty of Versailles is in tatters.

Czechoslovakia begins to mobilise its forces in May 1938 following reports of German military preparations. Britain and France send a stark warning to Germany – it does little.

The Munich Crisis, which followed in September, was widely viewed as the final prelude to all out war and allowed the Nazis to annex Czechoslovakia's Sudetenland.

A deal was negotiated in Munich by Britain, France, Italy and Germany, without the presence of Czechoslovakia.

British Prime Minister Chamberlain thought Hitler would be satisfied if his demands were met; he even returned home a hero after he got the Nazi leader to sign a peace treaty.

Dorothy Welsby: "It was so awful to see Europe sliding back into war once more. Hitler would stop at nothing to get more land for the new Germany, a country that was re-arming at a frightening rate and no one was stopping them.

"I remember watching the newsreel of Chamberlain looking jubilant as he waved his paper in the air getting off the plane. We all hoped he'd achieved peace in our time, as he told us, but I don't think anyone really believed it.

"It wasn't long before our worst fears had been confirmed and we were at war once again." Conscription was introduced in Britain the same month.

Joyce Green: "We were very traumatised by the rise of Nazism. You knew that something was going to happen eventually. You knew there was a war coming. Secretly I think we were all afraid of what that would bring."

The front page headline of The Star on Thursday, August 31, 1939, left Sheffielders in no doubt of the state of play: 'Evacuation of schools will begin tomorrow' it said.

Germany invaded Poland the following day.

On September 2, a British ultimatum was sent to Germany demanding a withdrawal.

Adolf Hitler, Hermann Goering, Julius Streicher and other senior members of the German Nazi Party in November 1938 prior to the outbreak of hostilities

---

DOROTHY WELSBY:
"**There can't be many people that haven't heard Chamberlain's broadcast that was originally heard at 11.15am on September 3, 1939.**

"**You could have heard a pin drop at the time – it was the same right across the country. There was a feeling of absolute dread when he announced there'd been no withdrawal.**

"**Sheffield and the country was now officially at war.**"

It might be YOU!

CARING FOR EVACUEES IS A NATIONAL SERVICE

ISSUED BY THE MINISTRY OF HEALTH

CHAPTER FOUR
Walking back from Leicester - Sheffield prepares for the worst...

A barrage balloon on Crookesmoor Recreation ground

There's no doubt the casualty toll would have been infinitely higher had the Sheffield Blitz come earlier in the war.

Over a year had passed since the outbreak of hostilities; Sheffield had been working flat out to protect its citizens and its munitions industry that was such an integral part of the fight back against the Nazis.

As such a vital part of the UK's war effort many were surprised the air attack took so long to arrive.

Evacuation plans were drawn up for cities that were deemed key targets months before – Sheffield was one of them.

In July 1939 several key cities held evacuation rehearsals.

By September the real thing had started in earnest, but the numbers actually moved varied vastly from place to place.

Only 15% of children from Sheffield ended up being evacuated.

Rail operator LNER organised 20 trains to leave Sheffield Victoria Station with the city's children bound for destinations such as Newark, Bingham and Loughborough. Many of the trains ended up being only a third full.

The 135 children from Carbrook Council School were taken to Leicestershire and billeted in five villages set several miles apart.

The task of keeping contact between the isolated groups was down to various teachers in cars.

Three hundred kids from Abbeydale School were sent to Loughborough.

Evacuation coincided with Germany's attack on Poland and many cities called for a second thrust to encourage greater numbers.

The reaction in Sheffield was less than encouraging.

BARRAGE BALLOONS
One of the most visible signs of war in Sheffield was the floating of scores of huge balloons above the city to defend against aircraft attacking at low level. Special barrage balloon units were formed as part of the Auxiliary Air Force. Over 1,000 people volunteered. They launched 72 balloons on the first night of the Sheffield Blitz.

Sheffield's date with Hitler

Sheffield children are evacuated from the city's Victoria Station

On September 11 city schools were taking names of prospective evacuees.

Thirty five minutes after the opening of registration at Queen Street's Cathedral School there'd not been a single name put forward.

The parents of Haydn Anderson were typical of many in the close-knit community of Attercliffe – an area that was always going to be a likely target for attack because of the high density of steel works.

He said: "The evacuation procedure was voluntary for children of school age. They'd be taken off into rural areas, to live in with families there. Fortunately, neither mine, nor any of the parents where we lived, took up this option. I would have been mortified."

Incredibly, by October 1939, evacuees had actually begun to arrive back in Sheffield.

In one case a 7 and a 9-year-old started walking back from Leicester.

They ended up hitch-hiking and arrived back in Sheffield the same day.

ARP volunteers

Another vital part of the city's defences were the ARP (Air Raid Precaution) volunteers.

Around 80% were unpaid and already had full time jobs. One in six were women.

It was their job to judge the extent of any air raid damage and advise on the type and size of rescue services to send out.

They also had to organise the movement of the "bombed out" to safety in another shelter.

They masterminded literally hundreds of drills in Sheffield as the population braced itself for anything from gas attacks to wide-scale bombing.

A massive exercise – involving 1,300 wardens – took place in the run up to war in November 1938 for example.

Hundreds of incidents were staged across the ARP's Sheffield southern division including gas bombs, high explosive bombs and damage to roads, electric cables and water mains.

A warden sounds a rattle to announce the discovery of gas during a November 1938 exercise

Protection courtesy of Sir John Anderson

Anderson Shelters were the protection of choice for most people in the city.

Named after Sir John Anderson, Secretary of State for Home Affairs, they became a familiar site in gardens and backyards.

Over 2 million were distributed free of charge to citizens but in October 1939 the Government decided anyone earning over £5 a week had to buy their own.

Anderson Shelters were cheap to produce and were capable of protecting up to six people from almost anything bar a direct hit.

Many people made them feature pieces of their gardens.

In Sheffield, 58 public buildings were modified to allow them to be used as communal air raid shelters in existing cellars and vaults.

There were also a further 294 shelters provided by shops, pubs, banks and other buildings in places requisitioned for war use.

Other large shelters were purpose built.

Many communal shelters had full time wardens and first aid posts and developed their own social life through regular concerts, sing songs and so forth.

The search for tunnels, cellars, basement storage rooms, mine shafts, and anything else that could be conceivably be converted into an air raid shelter was begun as early as 1938, as war was looking more and more likely.

The Furnival Road arches, then part of the approach to Sheffield Victoria Station, which shut in early 1970s, were earmarked for possible conversion into shelters.

THIS IS STEEL CITY

Pictures of searchlights and anti-aircraft gun sites appeared regularly in the Sheffield press in 1939 to help reassure people they were being kept safe.

When War Minister, Leslie Hore-Belisha, visited Sheffield as part of a tour of the region he told a journalist: "This is a steel city. A most important city. It is ringed with defences of steel."

The defences were soon to be tested to the limit.

SHEFFIELD DECOYS

Bombing decoys were constructed on Strines and Burbage Moors and in Eckington Woods in a bid to confuse the German bombers.

The massive operation involved strategically placing oil tanks filled with oil, shavings and tin foil that were to be set alight to act as decoys.

Top: Sheffielders prepare their Anderson Shelters

Above: A shelter is turned into a centre-piece for this particular Sheffield garden on Mushroom Lane

Far left: Furnival Road arches were earmarked for ARP services prior to the out-break of hostilities

Sheffield's date with Hitler

By September 1939 a number of boards coated with gas sensitized paint had been placed at strategic points around the city

The introduction of a blackout was one of the biggest and most immediate signs of a city at war.

Though it was seen as a big success it brought about unforeseen hazards as Sheffielders attempted to navigate a city in total darkness.

In January 1940 a total of 14 people died on the roads in the blackout.

The death toll caused a rethink and the following month a modified blackout was introduced.

Street lighting reappeared but on a vastly reduced basis; it was also hooded so it couldn't be seen from the air.

The defence of Sheffield was the responsibility of a new civilian army being mobilised following an appeal on May 14, 1940, by Sir Anthony Eden – then Secretary of State for War.

He asked all men aged between 17 and 65 to form the new force to guard factories, railways, canals and other vital points and prepare for any invading German troops.

The first man had come forward to volunteer in Sheffield within four minutes of the broadcast.

The new army was originally titled the Local Defence Volunteers but was later renamed the Home Guard and immortalised years later in the popular 'Dad's Army' series.

But far from being the disorganised bunch of incompetents portrayed in the TV programme, the Sheffield Home Guard battalions were a vital part of the city's defence.

Many of them were already trained soldiers who had fought for the country in WW1.

Rationing

Chancellor of the Exchequer, Sir John Simon, firmly brought the war effort into every home in Sheffield on September 27, 1939, with the unveiling of his Emergency War Budget.

Petrol was the first commodity to be rationed and duties were increased on everything from tobacco to sugar to raise funds.

In January meat and basic foodstuffs were rationed, but with the odd concession.

Extra cheese was allowed to workers with no canteen facilities and vegetarians got special dispensation, provided they handed over their meat coupons.

A 'points' system of rationing came into play for clothing and tinned meats.

Tinned salmon, crab, oranges, pineapples and lemon were not rationed because they were already nigh on impossible get hold of.

By 1942 Sir Stafford Cripps, Leader of the House of Commons, announced "personal extravagance must be eliminated altogether".

Women resorted to painting their legs with gravy browning as silk stockings became a thing of the past.

Cuts were made in clothing rations, sporting events were curtailed and pleasure motoring was banned.

Haydn Anderson was lucky enough to get the odd extra.

He said: "Dad worked in the coal industry for the Brightside and Carbrook Co-operative and was deemed to be in a reserved occupation, so he was not called up for armed service. He also did all night 'fire-watching duty' at the Co-op's grocery store, which is probably why we got one or two extras at times."

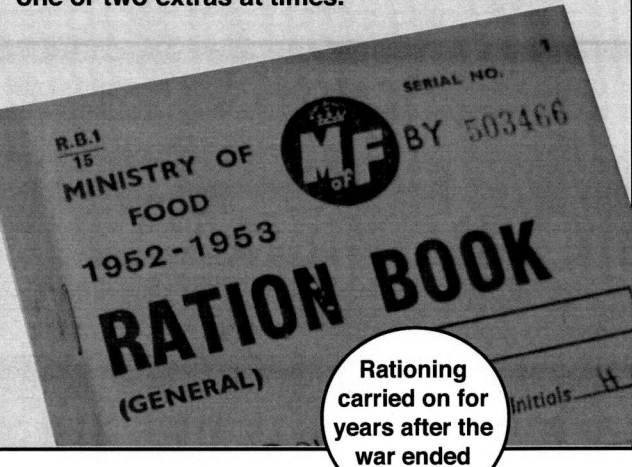

Rationing carried on for years after the war ended

CHAPTER FIVE
"It's an air raid not a damn jumble sale" - life in the Anderson Shelter

Soldiers march past the Lord Mayor in Barker's Pool

Though Anderson Shelters offered protection from bombs, they did little to stop neighbourhood disputes.

In fact hours spent enduring the idiosyncrasies of families next door would regularly blow up into massive rows.

The problem stemmed from the communal nature of many shelters, set up to house more than one family.

The goings-on inside the one at the back of 45 Coningsby Road, Firvale, were typical of events being played out across the city.

Harold Hickson, a Sheffield City Battalion veteran; one of the few to make it back virtually unscathed from the Battle of the Somme in WW1, was normally the peace maker according to his daughter.

Dorothy Welsby said: "The war years took their toll, but we also had many laughs.

"My father diligently erected an Anderson Shelter in the back yard, complete with sleeping bunks, paraffin lamp and rugs on the floor. My mother had a case in which she kept important insurance documents; on hearing the sirens, everyone would make a rush for the shelter, father always bringing up the rear, complete with case. We four, including my very young daughter Patricia, had to fit ourselves into a very small space to make room for the others.

"Next door to us lived a very volatile family, consisting of a mother and daughter. They would join us, better equipped for a holiday than an air raid. The daughter always arrived first, face caked in mudpack, hair in rollers and carrying a huge suitcase and umpteen shoe boxes.

"The mother followed on, also hair in rollers. She always sported an enormous polythene bag of new vests and undies.

Sheffield's date with Hitler

Marching up Fargate and past Sheffield Town Hall

Audrey Eaton

"Over her arms she carried various frocks and coats. It was a work of art getting them into the shelter at all.

"My dad, who was normally the peace maker, used to get that wound up he used to say: 'What the devil have you brought all this for, it's more like a damned jumble sale than an air raid."

"When they finally settled down the mother would say to the daughter: 'Have you got your best coat?'. And the daughter would answer: 'No, you said you'd bring it', whereupon the mother would reply: 'That must have been it that I was walking on inside the doorway'.

"This would bring forth a torrent of abuse from the daughter. They'd call each other every vile name under the sun. This would go on until the mother retrieved the coat from the floor.

"My dad, even more wound up by now, would then shout: 'Don't you dare bring another damned thing into this shelter.'

"The mother used to take great affront to this but, bizarrely, her look of absolute thunder used to send her daughter into absolute fits of laughter to which the mother charmingly replied 'Shut your mouth or I'll knock your flaming head off'.

"It's fair to say the relief at the all clear sirens was far more to do with getting out of the way of this pair.

"It wouldn't end there but at least, out of the shelter, we'd got a brick wall between us.

"Once inside the house we'd hear an ungodly commotion next door as crockery started flying.

"I remember one morning the mother staggered into the yard shouting: 'That bastard has just hit me with a chair.'"

Many houses in Sheffield had their cellars reinforced so they could act as air raid protection and doors installed to allow quick access to neighbouring property if the worst happened.

But Audrey Eaton, who was living in Attercliffe at the time, recalls that the work was still to be done when war broke out.

"I was 15 when the war started in 1939. I remember when the air raid sirens started for the first time properly – there'd been a few try outs but this was the first proper one to signal an attack. Well it was a right carry on. They hadn't built shelters and things and I don't think our cellar had been reinforced, so we had to go to Oaks Green Wash House because they'd got one there.

CUT OUT THIS "DIRECTORY" OF AIR RAID SHELTERS

IN order that our readers may familiarise themselves with public air raid shelters in bus and tram route areas a list will be published in "The Star" each day showing shelters erected in the Sheffield area.

The list given below shows those in the central area of the city, and on ...nday the first section of shelters on or near the tramway routes will be given.

It is stressed that these shelters are provided for persons who may be caught in the streets and not within easy reach of their own homes.

On no account should people leave their homes to seek shelter in a public shelter.

Readers should cut out the lists appearing in "The Star" and acquaint themselves with the location of the shelters on or near the routes by which they usually travel.

Master keys for the shelters are held by all wardens and police officers, but in the event of there being no such authorised person available when an air raid warning is sounded, any member of the public may break the glass in the small illuminated boxes near the door and use the key contained therein to open the shelter.

PUBLIC AIR RAID SHELTERS IN CENTRAL AREA

Address	Occupier	Capacity
ALDINE COURT, High Street, adapted passage		30
ANGEL STREET, Jay's		350
ARUNDEL STREET, No. 63, Wiggins and Co.		88
ARUNDEL STREET, No. 137, Milner		60
ARUNDEL STREET, No. 195, B. Worth and Son		110
BACKFIELDS, St. Matthew's School		112
BAILEY STREET, Cook and Co.		35
BALM GREEN, Grand Garage		450
BANK STREET, No. 45-47, Neale's Chambers		400
BARKER'S POOL, Albert Hall		200
BOWER SPRING, Surface shelter		40
BROAD LANE, No. 114, Robertson and Russell		45
BROOMHALL STREET, Surface shelter		40
BROOMHALL STREET, No. 89/91, T. Earnshaw and Co.		50
BROOMSPRING LANE, No. 47/63, Freeman Oakes, Ltd.		300
BUTTON LANE, Surface shelter		40
CAMBRIDGE STREET, Handsworth Motor Co.		420
CAMPO LANE, Cathedral		130
CANNING STREET, Surface shelter		40
CARVER STREET, No. 35, C. Constantine, Ltd.		130
CASTLE STREET, Court House		250
CASTLE STREET, Exchange Cafe		250
CASTLE STREET, No. 12-14, E. Miller		110
CHARLES STREET, Sheffield Sports Hall		200
CHURCH STREET, No. 23-25, A.R.P. Office		70
CHURCH STREET, Cathedral		70
CORPORATION STREET, No. 42, Windebank and Co., Ltd.		100
CUMBERLAND STREET, Surface shelter		40
CUMBERLAND STREET, Surface shelter		40
CUMBERLAND STREET, Surface shelter		40
DEVONSHIRE STREET, Surface shelter		40
DEVONSHIRE STREET, Nos. 140/146, Rowlands and Co.		180
DIVISION STREET, No. 66-68, Z. Butterwick and Co.		50
EARL STREET CAR PARK (Porter Street, Eyre Street, Jessop Street), Trench		366
ECCLESALL ROAD, Old Albion Brewery		150
EXCHANGE STREET, Norfolk Market Hall		525
EYRE LANE, No. 28, K. Brody		35
FARGATE, empty shops corner, Leopold Street		40
FARGATE, No. 33-35, J. Woodhouse and Son		175
FARGATE (Y.M.C.A., Blg.), Bradwell Bros., Dr. Scholls, W. May, Ltd.		200
FARGATE, No. 20-30, Proctors, Ltd.		93
FAVELL ROAD, No. 14, Dr. Robertson		52
FAWCETT STREET, No. 90-92, Bellefield Hotel		45
FAWCETT STREET, No. 88, Sheffield and Ecclesall Co-op. Society		52
FITZWILLIAM STREET, No. 36A, H. Hill		60
FURNIVAL LANE, Tunnel adjoining Sheffield Cabinet Company		200
GELL STREET, No. 34, Rev. DAWSON Parsons		115
GLOSSOP ROAD, No. 257, Jameson and Co.		90
GLOSSOP ROAD, No. 266, A. Mackay		50
HIGH STREET, Modes C. and A., Ltd.		200
HIGH STREET, No. 43, Samuels and Sweard and Wells		355
HIGH STREET, No. 19, Bell and Co.		100
HOWARD STREET, No. 15-27, Empire Trading Co.		
JERICHO STREET, No. 85, Wilde, Ltd.		
KING STREET, No. 23, Colver and Company		
LEADMILL ROAD, No. 81, F. Crapper		
LOVE STREET, E. Dixon		
MEADOW STREET, Meadow Buildings		
MILLSANDS, Tennant's Brewery		260
MILTON STREET, No. 44, Thos. Hardy		96
THE MOOR, No. 138, Wyn's		100
THE MOOR, No. 81-85, Price and Crowes		150
THE MOOR, No. 35, Weaver to Wearer		100
THE MOOR, No. 27 and 29, Nipp's Ltd. and Mays		60
THE MOOR, No. 190A-192, Haris (Wallpaper) Haris (Footwear), Ltd.		160
MOORE STREET, Surface shelter		40
MOORE STREET, Surface shelter		40
MOORE STREET, Surface shelter		40
MOOR STREET/FITZWILLIAM ST., Trench		300
MOORHEAD, Devonshire Arms		155
NEWCASTLE STREET, Trench		219
NORFOLK LANE, No. 23, Truswell's Brewery		290
NORFOLK STREET, Congregational Church		200
NORTH CHURCH STREET, R. Stiring and Sons		132
NURSERY STREET, Lion Hotel		300
ORCHARD STREET, Sunshine Foods, Ltd.		150
PINSTONE STREET, 90/2, T. J. Batchelor, Ltd.		200
POND STREET, Surface shelter		40
POND STREET (under Gallimore's premises) (top of steps) opp. Bus Station		90
POND STREET, Rawson's Brewery		108
POND STREET GOODS STATION, L.M.S. Railway Arches		140
POND STREET AND FLAT STREET JUNCTION (Tramway shelter), Sandbag surface shelter		70
PORTER STREET, Trench		350
PORTER STREET, Surface shelter		50
QUEEN STREET, No. 185, W.		120

"It was absolutely hilarious. There was my mother, my sister Barbara and me at home – the rest of the family must have been out. My mother had got a pair of my sister's high heel shoes on and she'd got them on the wrong feet. One of the neighbour's sons was complaining that he couldn't find his trousers and his mother shouted, 'never mind your trousers, get your coat on'.

"One of our Irene's neighbours was shouting to her daughter 'to get the insurance policies from under the sink'. And I said 'why couldn't she come and get them'? Apparently she was stood petrified at the stop of the stairs and her legs wouldn't move!"

AIR RAID INSTRUCTIONS
ISSUED TO..........
The man who hands you this card is an
AIR RAID WARDEN
BE CALM:- LIE FLAT ON YOUR BACK.
IMPORTANT: Do whatever the warden tells you.

BEFORE, DURING AND AFTER THE RAID No. 1

KEEPING WARM AND COMFORTABLE IN YOUR SHELTER

—and the help that is ready if your home is hit

If you are sleeping in an Anderson or brick surface shelter, every extra bit of immediate comfort and convenience that you can arrange in your shelter makes it easier for you to stand up to the bombing. Here are some hints taken from leaflets which are being issued to all shelterers by local authorities.

THE EARLY EVENING
For reading or knitting a good light is necessary. Try a candle, lamp or nightlights. These are good for the eyes. Oil lamps are dangerous, as they may get spilled by shock from bombs. They make the air foul, too. If you do use one, be sure to put it out before going to sleep.

HEATING
Never have a coke or other brazier in the shelter. They give off dangerous fumes. Oil stoves are also a source of danger, as they use up the oxygen which you need for breathing. A candle heater is useful. Put the candle in a flowerpot, and then put a second flowerpot over the top. Raise the lower pot slightly from the ground. Try a hot water bottle or a hot brick in the bed. Heat the brick in the oven for two hours, first and wrap it up.

GETTING TO SLEEP
A warm drink helps, particularly with children. Remember that when you are not sleeping on a thick mattress you need as much underneath you as on top. Have a good thick layer of newspapers, or brown paper, to lie on. Paper is draught proof. It is most important that bedding should be thoroughly aired every day.

IN THE NIGHT
Have something to eat, such as sweets or biscuits. Keep plenty of warm outdoor clothes beside you, in case you have to go out of the shelter. If you feel a draught, hang a curtain in front of the bunk. Wear your ear plugs.

IF YOUR HOUSE IS HIT
Make your plans about what to do. Arrange now to go and stay with friends or relations – and for them to come to you if their house suffers. If you can't make such plans, find out where your Emergency Rest Centre is. There you will be given food, shelter, clothes and money if necessary, and a billet will be found for you.

Help is ready
If your income is below a certain amount, you can apply to the Assistance Board for a grant to replace essential furniture and household goods, or tools essential for your work if you lose them through bombing.

ISSUED BY THE MINISTRY OF HOME SECURITY

Petre Street Barrage balloon site

Young Sheffield firewatcher Norman Hickson

Haydn Anderson was relieved that his goldfish survived the attacks.

He said: "The war years must have been a very worrying time for parents, but they certainly didn't transfer any of their fears to us. The sound of the sirens was alarming, but we got used to it and were convinced the German bombers would never find us; even though the broadcasts of Lord Haw-Haw [New York-born William Joyce who became infamous for leading Germany's radio propaganda service aimed at UK listeners throughout the war] told us otherwise.

"Dad said our Anderson Shelter was the safest on the street, having piled loads and loads of earth on top.

"There were top and bottom bunks on either side and a little paraffin stove near the door. I remember well the smell of the stove and the hessian sacking on the bunks to this day. We were really a prime target, with the steel works of Brown Bayleys at the bottom of the road which was hit on the second night of the Sheffield Blitz, a canal aqueduct and the railway lines close by. I remember houses were hit a couple of streets away, near the works, and after that night in the shelter I found all our windows had been shattered. Not a drop was spilled from the goldfish bowl I was amazed to find.

"The propaganda machine was in full swing and we all knew who the baddies were. Hitler and his henchmen, Himmler, Goering, Goebbels and Hess were heartily despised.

"One of the tales related to me by my parents was about the time Uncle Lawrence, my mother's younger brother, came home on leave, and was staying with us. There was an air raid and we all had to spend the night in the shelter. You could always tell when it was a German bomber overhead – they had a different sound. So when I picked up the sound of one, I apparently called up to my uncle, saying –

"'Uncle Lol, can you hear 'em.

"'Hear what?' he said.

"'Them Germans Uncle Lol; its that bloody Goering! He'll drop his bloody bombs and then he'll bugger off home'.

"I'd have been no more than four years old."

Sheffield's date with Hitler

45

Lord Mayor Alderman J. A. Longdon takes the salute from Sheffield wardens outside Sheffield Town Hall

Wings For Victory Week at Owler Lane

Sheffield ATC (Air Training Corps) cadets at Stephenson Hall

Member of Sheffield NFS (National Fire Service) taking messages

CHAPTER SIX
The munitions industry and Sheffield's Women of Steel

Looking in disbelief at the damage

The Germans were acutely aware of Sheffield's pivotal role in the country's war effort. The city's steelworks turned out the raw materials and munitions that kept much of the country's armed forces fighting.

Sheffield's steelworks and foundries were targets for the hundreds of raiders that pounded the city on December 12 and 15, 1940.

But despite causing damage to the industrial heartland of the city, Hitler totally failed to stop it.

The Luftwaffe could have done irreparable damage to the country's war effort if they'd have hit the English Steel Corporation's Vickers works in the city's East End.

This was home to the only hammer in the land capable of turning out crankshafts for Rolls-Royce Merlin engines, fitted to Spitfire and Hurricane aircraft that won the Battle of Britain.

48 | Sheffield's date with Hitler

Mary, Sally, Marie and Edith, the only female gang of platelayers in the North of England, working in Sheffield

Buffer girls enjoying a mobile refreshments centre in December, 1940

Manned by a crew of 16, the beats of the 15 ton dropped hammer could be heard for miles around.

The nation's tank regiments also owed a huge thanks to Sheffield.

Steelworkers produced 872 Matilda tank turrets, another 515 for Churchill tanks and a further 116,743 tank components.

As in WW1, just a few years earlier, women were once again called upon

As in WW1, just a few years earlier, women were once again called upon to undertake a wide variety of jobs. Single women between the ages of 19 and 24 were called up and given the choices of women's services, Civil Defence, and civilian jobs deemed essential to the war effort.

By the end of the war there were at least 260,000 women working in munitions factories and a further 770,000 in engineering and vehicle building.

They stepped into thousands of roles left empty as men were sent to fight overseas.

Women kept South Yorkshire's steelworks producing vital bullets and parts for guns, tanks, ships and planes as war raged across Europe.

They were vital in keeping transport systems operating.

The railways initially employed women as porters, carters, van drivers and ticket collectors, but as war progressed and the railways as a whole lost 100,000 men to the armed forces, women were trained as passenger guards, electricians, fitters, boiler cleaners, painters, blacksmiths and more.

Women's wages rose more than men's and in some trades a move was made towards equal pay but, in engineering, the average woman's pay was only half that of her male counterpart.

Many were just teenagers when they were sent to work through air raids in terrifying conditions in the foundries of the region.

Some of the WVS members making brushes for work use

Sheffield's date with Hitler

Sheffield Bureau

A captured miniature German sub on view on Carver Street

Sheffield's Date with Hitler

The navy gives a hand as 250,000 new allotments are started to help the war effort – this one is in Sheffield

They worked alongside women from a myriad of professions not deemed necessary to the war effort.

Many pregnant workers took just a week off before returning to work with their tiny babies left in a nearby nursery – with every break taken used to feed their newly born children.

Accidents were a daily hazard: hair being ripped out by machines; scars from molten metals splashing onto their skin; broken bones from falls down crane ladders and doing jobs so important they couldn't stop even if German bombs were falling all around.

Many loved their new-found roles, other hated every minute.

Women from middle-class backgrounds were regularly bullied for being snobs and were shocked by the colourful language and attitudes of the hardened steelmen.

But together they supported each other through tragedy and built up an amazing

But together they supported each other through tragedy and built up an amazing camaraderie which made it all the harder to accept the way they were treated at the end of the war.

camaraderie which made it all the harder to accept the way they were treated at the end of the war.

With men returning home, the women who had kept the steelworks running were fired without a word of thanks.

Some were given five days warning that their stint was about to end forever; others turned up to work to find a man next to their machine.

Seventy years on and their amazing efforts are finally being officially recognised by Government and The Star's high profile 'Women of Steel' campaign.

52 Sheffield's date with Hitler

Walsh's store is turned into a raging inferno on High Street

A tram lays in bits on The Wicker

CHAPTER SEVEN
The Sheffield Blitz - the city's worst fears come true

Sheffield's air raid early warning system followed a distinct, colour-coded pattern. A yellow alert was the first sign of danger, this moved to purple as the sign of threat increased and the sirens sounded at code red signalling an imminent attack.

Air raid sirens were nothing new over the city of Sheffield by December 1940 – there'd already been countless false alarms and drills which had started months before hostilities even began.

There'd also been actual air raids which were later seen as reconnaissance missions for the devastation to come.

Blackbrook Road, for example, was hit in August, 1940, with no casualties. A raid on Sheaf Street the same month amassed the first fatalities – four people killed and a further 78 injured.

But nothing could have prepared the city for the blitzkrieg of 'Operation Crucible' – the German code name for the two-nights of absolute carnage that saw around 300 Luftwaffe bombers unleashing living hell in an attempt to pound Sheffield into submission.

Aftermath of the first night of the Sheffield Blitz looking towards the remains of C & A Modes (the area now occupied by Primark)

54 — Sheffield's date with Hitler

Devastation on an unimaginable scale on King Street

Sheffield's date with Hitler

It was late in the afternoon on Thursday, December 12, 1940, that British monitoring stations detected the first tell tale signs of another German air raid.

X-Gerat radio beams had once again been found being laid across Northern England with the intention of guiding Hitler's deadly bombers to another intended target.

Intelligence staff were immediately on a race against the clock to work out the likeliest target of the invisible beams in order to give as much warning as possible to get people to safety.

Though they discovered the beams pointed to Sheffield – the very heart of the UK's industrial war effort – there was still no guarantee at this stage that the bombers would actually strike and, if they did, there was no knowing of the planned size and severity of the attack.

At 6.15pm that night the early warning system was put at code yellow confirming an attack was looking likely.

By 6.45pm it had moved a notch to purple with the public at large still unaware that anything was wrong.

At 7pm the early warning system had reached code red and the air raid sirens roared into life over Sheffield as some kind of attack was on its way.

German maps for the Luftwaffe pilots showed a Sheffield raid had been planned in meticulous detail.

At 7pm the early warning system had reached code red and the air raid sirens roared into life over Sheffield as some kind of attack was on its way

The destruction of key factories, railway lines, bridges and roads were key to inflicting massive damage – strategic targets were clearly highlighted on the maps of Sheffield carried by each plane.

Sheffielders – blissfully unaware there was wave after wave of German bomber either leaving or preparing to leave occupied Northern France and head north to Steel City at this point - weren't particularly unnerved by the 7pm wailing sirens.

Blitz damage on Bocking Lane

56 — Sheffield's date with Hitler

Angel Street in ruins

The end of the road for this Church Army Mobile canteen

It was nothing they'd not heard before and there'd been enough false alarms to make many people quite blasé about them.

In any case it was half-day closing on a Thursday and the city was trying hard to replace talk of war with pre-Christmas frivolities.

In a matter of minutes the first enemy planes were heard approaching Sheffield that night along with a sound that wasn't so familiar - the distant thud of anti-aircraft fire

There was plenty of opportunity for a bit of normality that night: a dance was underway at the Cutlers' Hall; Henry Hall was set to perform at the Empire Theatre; Bernard Taylor and his band were playing at Sheffield City Hall; Blue Bird starring Shirley Temple was on offer at the Central Cinema and 'Saps at Sea' starring Laurel and Hardy was been screened at the Regent Cinema and the city centre's bars, restaurants and hotels were gearing up for one of the busiest nights of the year.

Unfortunately – or fortunately as it felt for many in hindsight – not everyone had the opportunity to join the thousands heading into town for a party that night: steelworkers were busy clocking on in the East End for a 12 hour night shift.

In a matter of minutes the first enemy planes were heard approaching Sheffield that night together with a sound that wasn't so familiar – the distant thud of anti-aircraft fire from their vantage points around the city.

They arrived in the shape of pathfinder units from Kampfgruppe 100 acting in advance of the massive German military might of the Luftwaffe thundering its way north on the frosty December night.

Heinkel III aircraft dropped their first incendiaries and parachute flares to pinpoint targets over the residential suburbs of Norton Lees and Gleadless.

The aftermath of the Sheffield Blitz in a suburb

Wilfred Welsby:

"By this time many people in the suburbs believed this was going to be a bad raid. Something in the air felt very wrong that night. We were in our Anderson shelters within minutes."

People caught out away from their homes started looking for the nearest public shelter.

Following in the slipstream of the first raiders were three groups of German aircraft lined up to unleash nine hours of relentless bombing over the city via the dropping of 350 tons of high explosives.

By 7.30pm houses at Brincliffe Edge, Woodseats, Abbeydale, Glossop Road and Park Hill were a blazing inferno.

The first wave of high explosives had fallen in a line across Oakhill Road, Moncrieffe Road, and Westbrook Bank at Nether Edge and Sharrow.

More devastating incendiaries followed in their wake.

There was soon a ring of fire connecting Intake, Woodseats, Millhouses, Sharrow, Broomhill, Crookesmoor, Walkley, Owlerton and Burngreave.

Bombs also started to fall on the city centre.

Just before 8pm the police ordered the mass evacuation of key leisure establishments with audiences directed to public shelters.

From that point on the raid got worse with a deadly mix of incendiaries and high explosive bombs raining down on the city.

A shower of incendiary bombs fell on the Sheffield and District Gas Company at Neepsend, one of them puncturing a gas holder.

One brave employee stemmed the large sheet of flame shooting from the hole with a mix of clay and asbestos after the third attempt.

Destruction on a massive scale spread through Neepsend, Philadelphia and Pye Bank.

By this time the situation in the city centre was getting steadily worse with many people who had originally taken refuge in nearby public shelters decided it was safer to make an escape for the suburbs.

Indiscriminate bombing made it feel like no one and nowhere was safe, which was always at the core of Hitler's planning.

Three direct hits were scored on Nether Edge Hospital with one ward wrecked and five patients killed. One expectant mother gave birth to her baby whilst laying under a bed for protection.

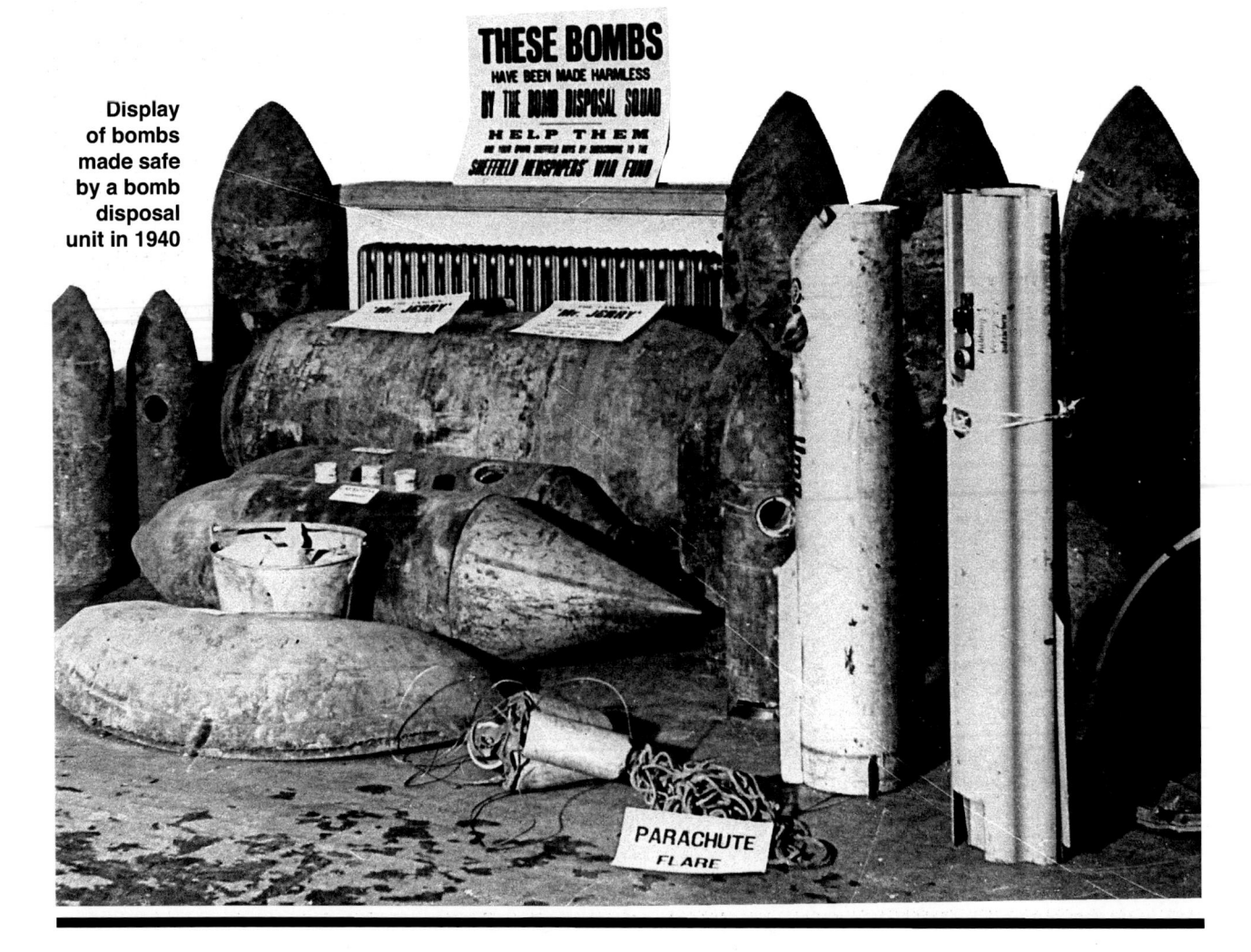

Display of bombs made safe by a bomb disposal unit in 1940

Sheffield's date with Hitler

The Moor

The worst part of the attack that night came between 11pm and 1am with the heaviest loss of life in any single incident taking place at the Marples Hotel in Fitzalan Square.

Incendiary bombs set fire to the Electricity Department's workshops in Commercial Street, and a high explosive bomb hit the works of George Senior next door, bringing down an enormous chimney which flattened other buildings as it felt.

The bombing turned the city centre into a raging inferno of unthinkable proportions.

Only hours earlier the shops of King Street and Angel Street had been bustling with Christmas shoppers. By 4am on Friday, December 13, 1940, there wasn't a single premises that wasn't completely destroyed or on fire.

Cockaynes department store was a mass of flames and crumbling masonry. The beautiful HL Brown jewellers was totally wiped out. The old Angel Hotel – which gave Angel Street its name – was a ball of flames.

Once mighty tramcars had been tossed around like rag dolls, split in two and burning furiously.

NELLIE BENNETT: "I can remember sirens going. We lived opposite Ellesmere Rd School. We spent Blitz night in the boiler house of the school. They kept bringing people in while the bombs kept dropping.

"The Salvation Army came and brought sandwiches."

LILLEY CROSSLAND: "My father worked on Attercliffe Common and he came home as the sirens were going.

"It was just a few days before Christmas and trams were already on fire so he had to walk most of the way home to Malin Bridge."

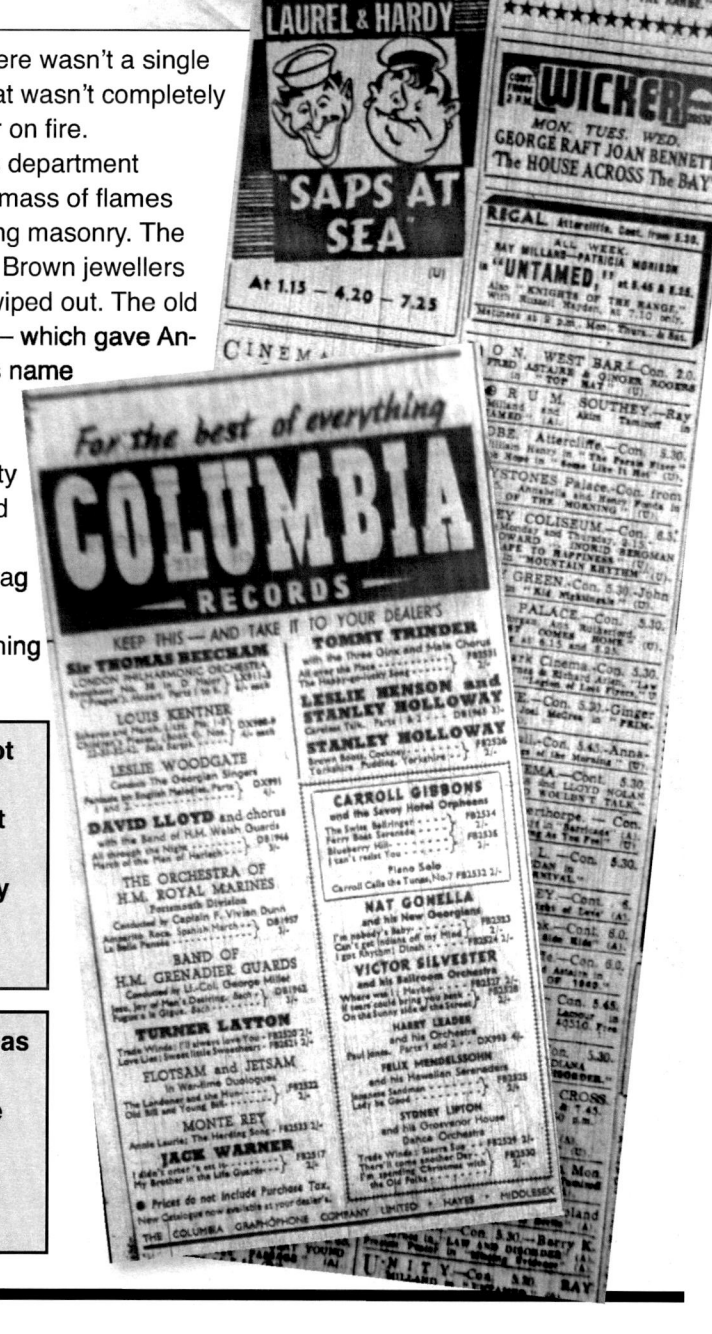

The Moor was one of the worst areas hit – it was bombed and virtually burnt out of existence.

Shopping institutions like Atkinsons, Marks & Spencer and Robert Brothers were gone in the blink of an eye.

Mr Christopher Eyre, who was driving a fire vehicle at the time, said: "We had been fighting a fire at the Empire [sited just off the top of The Moor] for more than an hour. Then bombs started falling all along The Moor. It's almost impossible to describe it – we could hear the whistling and the crashing, we were ringed in by the flames, and yet I seemed to be in a vacuum."

Despite the immense tragedy that saw whole families wiped out as they sheltered together in the suburbs there were also tales of incredible bravery and sheer luck.

Fargate escaped the carnage virtually unscathed. So did Sheffield Town Hall. A 600 pound bomb landed just yards from Sheffield City Hall. Fortunately it landed in an emergency water tank which cushioned the blast.

The iconic building survived bar the scars of flying shrapnel that can still be seen on the Corinthian pillars at the entrance.

The all clear was finally sounded at 4.17am on Friday, December 13.

Many compared it to the aftermath of an earthquake as people started to emerge from their shelters.

Sheffield lay stricken, almost paralysed with landmarks wiped off the skyline and families starting the harrowing task of searching for loved ones.

The Sheffield population, though shocked and temporarily dazed, showed incredible mettle and did not lose their heart or nerve. Far from breaking their spirit, it left them more determined than ever before to get behind the war effort and beat Hitler once and for all.

Damage to Bramall Lane

Three days respite and the Luftwaffe returned

The fires were still smouldering and teams were still searching for the dead and wounded when the planes returned for a second raid on Sunday, December 15. This time the East End came seriously under fire.

Incendiaries lit a path from Arbourthorne to Rotherham and Prince of Wales Road became a path of fire.

But the big steel firms suffered comparatively little damage as the Attercliffe area was pounded.

Many like Brown Bayleys and Hadfields received hits, but it wasn't serious enough to affect production in any major way.

Local housewives stayed in the streets making tea for the firefighters and rescue teams. Many clawed at the rubble with their bare hands alongside the men.

At the works, volunteers fought incendiaries by smothering them with handfuls of sludge as they landed on the roofs.

Two more raids were planned on Sheffield between December 12 and December 15, 1940 – they were both cancelled.

The Germans did return a further 15 times but nothing ever compared with the first night of the Sheffield Blitz on December 12, 1940.

JOAN LEE:
"I lived at Handsworth. I remember we had a shelter in the garden. They dropped a big bomb in the school yard at Handsworth. We were facing the recreation ground and the incendiary bombs lit up the whole area like daylight. It was a terrible, terrible time – very traumatic."

ALICE MAY PARKIN:
"I worked at a cinema near where John Lewis is now. I was an usherette there and they moved us into the City Hall and they brought a big Ack Ack gun to where the soldiers' cenotaph is in Barker's Pool. We sat on some seats on one side and when it went off we found ourselves on the other side!

"I walked right through it. Past Marples, C&A and I was covered in water. My mother and father kept a pub, the Brown Cow, at the bottom of Corporation Street. I went down Nursery Street on my way there and I got into problems again as another bomb had dropped."

Birch Road in Attercliffe

The story of George Hennings – watchman at Robert Brothers, The Moor, on December 12 and 13, 1940

"Somehow, it seemed as if there was something ominous in the very air and I remarked to the men who assisted me, 'I think we are in for a spell of trouble. Get down to the air raid shelter!' In my opinion, the shelter was one of the best in Sheffield and able to stand the shock of anything which could take place that night. I compelled the men to stay there while I went round to turn off all electric lights and gas at the mains.

"Soon after this there was a terrific noise and I was apprehensive of great danger. Time passed quickly. It had not got to eight o'clock and I went onto the roof in search of incendiary bombs. This I had to do alone for those with me were terror stricken. From the roof I could see many fires. Near this very spot, at the top of Matilda Street, Wilson's the wholesale tobacconist's shop was well alight. Looking up Pinstone Street I could see Campbell's furniture store was a blazing mass, flames leaping many feet high. At this time there seemed to be plenty of water available. About this hour I took a group of firemen for some hot milk as they were nearly frozen. It was bitterly cold.

"Then we were informed that water was scarce and shortly afterwards it went off altogether for the night. What a tragedy! Sticking to my duty, I went back to the shop and for a brief period nothing exciting happened. Going on to the roof again, I could see all around - Heeley, Millhouses, Abbeydale - what a position. Here I was, helpless as a child, unable to do anything to avert disaster, which I felt sure would befall the very place I was in. Down below my men were wandering about demented with fear. I realised they could only be a hindrance to me and by no means a help, so I bade them go home. This they ventured to do, only to find that in some instances their homes has been blasted and destroyed by bombs and fire.

"Nine o'clock! The danger grew nearer and nearer and yet our store remained whole; so far as I could perceive there was no damage - not so much as a window cracked. Going to the front of the shop, about 9.30pm, I looked down The Moor and saw to my horror many shops and trams ablaze. Then I realised what a blitz meant to us in Sheffield. At this time there was very little wind stirring and the fires were confined to the bottom end of the Moor. I could hear bombs falling in the distance and see fires starting in many more districts. Back I went to the roof of our own store and remained there until midnight.

"Then I realised that I could feel in no way safe at such a height, with the possibility of every avenue of escape cut off. Just at this time I was hit by a piece of shrapnel. It must have been from a shell bursting in the air near our building. A coping stone bore marked evidence of this, for about two feet of stone was chipped out. Fortunately for me I wore my steel helmet. To say I was grateful is altogether too mild an expression.

"At about 12.30am, a great change took place - bombs fell (both fire bombs and explosive bombs) everywhere, or so it seemed. Everyone was in a state of excitement and, by this time, flames were steadily creeping up the Moor. A strong wind rose at this hour and fanned the blaze into something like fury. Debris was falling all around and our store got its first shock. A great tremor caused by a bomb exploding nearby blasted out our great windows. Glass and woodwork was flying around us like hail in a whirling storm. Happily, I escaped with just a few minor injuries, which a drop of iodine relieved for the moment

"At this period we became isolated from every power: gas, electricity and water.

Redgates toy shop turned into a raging inferno on The Moor

Sheffield's Date with Hitler

Worst of all, we could not use the power we had from a human source. The wind came up the Moor with a great force - like a hurricane, helping the flames along; yet it was bitterly cold. All the buildings were ablaze - Atkinsons, Darley's, Gebhart's, Langton's and many others. I, along with others, could only watch and wait in fear and trembling, wondering as to what would be our fate.

"Then I had a brainwave. If the store should remain whole, with the windows gone, the assistants would be cold. So I unlocked the doors and went in at the Arcade to fix the heating apparatus. Just before finishing, there was a great ominous rumbling noise. Another bomb dropped near and looking around, I saw to my surprise that the back of the parcel office and all the stairs had collapsed from the effect of a bomb which crashed near the bottom of Rockingham Street This caused much havoc in the neighbourhood. From this time onwards bombs of every type seemed to fall continuously. Standing outside, opposite our store, I saw many things happen around me which made me feel anything but brave, and yet, like a lad in the last war, I was "afraid to be afraid". It was all so frightful, so fiendishly indescribable.

"Firemen, Ambulance men, A.R.P. Wardens, and workers and all branches of the Civil Defence were doing their bit and doing it well. Many people were trapped in shelters under shops. Sulphur and burning materials made these untenable, and still everyone stuck to the job in hand, whilst destruction played its fiendish part.

The wind came up The Moor with a great force - like a hurricane, helping the flames along; yet it was bitterly cold

"At about 2am a very old man came across to me. He told me he was the watchman at Woolworths and whilst he was sitting in the cellar, a bomb about the size of a fire extinguisher came through the shop floor into the cellar. He coolly said, "I knelt down to examine it and head something ticking inside so thought I better come out of the premises.

"Woolworth's blew up at 2.30am. The bomb was a time bomb! If I had not advised the man to stay out, he would have gone back.

"At this time, a fire brigade officer and I went to the Central Picture Palace and got in touch with the water department by telephone, but we were given to understand the position was hopeless as to water supply, and still the work of destruction, both by fire and bombs, went on. At this time, the Germans were machine-gunning the Moorhead area.

"The Moor up to Rockingham Street was well alight. Atkinsons was burning furiously. I stood at the top of Matilda Street and wondered what would be the outcome. Near to me, a fireman had been blown across the road. When found he was badly wounded; his leg had been blown off. For six months he was in hospital. He is now employed in the Fire Office as a telephone operator. He has been fitted with an aluminium leg.

Damage to Sheffield Empire on the corner of Charles Street and Union Street

"And so the night went on. Many people who had little or no knowledge of the district were going about like frightened sheep. The landlord of the Monument Tavern, situated near the staff entrance, was talking to me at 3.30am having just come out of the cellar. Back of Button Lane, on our side, was alight at this period. Shortly after, what a change!

"Fletcher's furniture works, Binghams and Warmby's, Neville and Sons - all going up in smoke at one time. And yet, there was no sign of serious damage to our store. I walked round whenever I could, hoping for the best. Fear had left me and a state of peculiar unafraid mentality took possession of me.

"News of the disaster passed on from one part of the city to the other from time to time, and still there was no chance of water to extinguish the fires raging in the surrounding buildings. It was now dangerous to be in the open for debris and shrapnel was flying in all directions. The Moor was one huge mass of flames. Right and left, in most parts gas mains and electricity mains were torn up.

"Above our store, at 3.45am, Bray's and Binns, and the rest of the shops in Button Lane were well alight, starting one after the other. Redgates, part of Berry's Vaults, Woolworths, The Devonshire, and other places were going one after the other in explosion and fire. Rats and cats were fleeing in all directions, but never once did I see a dog the whole night through. Then our fate grew gradually nearer. Material in flames was flying up the Moor, helped by a wind like a hurricane. This blew through every window - and still we were unscathed.

"Just before 4am a sergeant fireman and I were standing by Burton's the Tailors looking up to our roof opposite. We saw small fires starting in the mantle and dressmaking workshop. We rushed across and for a time fought the flames with all the means at our disposal including extinguishers, sand and any water available. We succeeded in getting the fire out for a while. Soon after 4am we turned downstairs to see what else we could do. Looking through the mantle department we saw at the extreme end of the store, the millinery department, and all that end was enveloped in flames. We could do no more, for the heat was intense and the smoke was suffocating. We could only come out into the open, to watch from the other side.

"In ten minutes the whole building was one mass of flames. Fifty or more firemen were waiting to do their duty, but they were helpless - no water! Then about this time the "all clear" sounded. Our building went on burning. So far, no one had suffered from injury on our site.

"Many people were released from shelters in and around our district in the Moor area. Moving about the neighbourhood, one would be startled by a voice from a damaged shelter, or a cellar grate, asking if the "all clear" had sounded. And oh, what strange sights greeted us everywhere. Men and women blackened with soot and smoke and powder blast. Destruction, devastation, everywhere.

"And, by God's grace, here we were spared!"

Lifting an unexploded bomb at the end of Devonshire Street

Sheffield's date with Hitler

Broomgrove Nursing Home residents (from left to right) Joyce Green, Nellie Bennett, Joan Sykes and Lily Crossland looking at a map of where the bombs fell on Sheffield during the Blitz along with author Neil Anderson

A suburb in ruins and a poignant thanks to rescuers

Sheffield's date with Hitler

Adolf Hitler

German Messerschmidt 109 Plane brought down at Margate, September, 1940, shown on Albert Hall site, Barkers Pool, in aid of the Sheffield Newspapers War Fund.

CHAPTER EIGHT
The myths surrounding the Sheffield Blitz

Hitler addressing the Reichstag after invading Austria

Strict wartime censoring of news reporting created the perfect environment for paranoia. If you add to that the effectiveness of Germany's propaganda machine via Lord Haw Haw's 'Germany Calling' announcements it's not surprising the country was rife with rumour and half truths.

There are many persistent rumours surrounding the Sheffield Blitz.

One of the biggest conspiracy theories of WW2 was that Churchill knew that Coventry was to be attacked, but didn't evacuate the city as the information had come from top secret Enigma messages decoded by Bletchley Park

It was suggested he didn't want to alert the Nazis to the fact their radio messages were being read.

This myth around the Coventry bombing which took place just days before Sheffield has been disproved by many of the people on the front line of the electronic warfare battle, such as Professor RV Jones and even Churchill himself.

Much of the attacks on Sheffield were seen as inevitable because it was assumed the Nazis wanted to knock out the city's ability to play a key part in the war effort; the attacks have long since been deemed a failure in German eyes because the targets were largely missed.

There have also been schools of thought that have suggested the British 'bent' the German radio beams that guided bombers to their targets to divert them away from Sheffield's industrial East End into the city centre.

But Nazi bombing maps we unearthed actually put the munitions works down as secondary targets – primary targets included hospitals and educational establishments.

Many of these were hit which calls into question whether the bombing raids were actually far more successful than originally thought.

How the Luftwaffe found Steel City

Ian Cheetham: "Finding exactly how the German bombers found their way to Sheffield using radio beams, and the methods used by the British to stop them, is an intriguing story.

"Methods employed included 'Ruffians', borrowed medical equipment, the secret Enigma code-breakers at Bletchley Park and men in garden sheds lashed to the top of radio masts 300 feet high.

"Details about the existence of a type of Luftwaffe navigation beam was discovered early in the war when a well-placed German, sympathetic to Britain (allegedly mathematician and physicist Hans Ferdinand Mayer) posted papers detailing various German weapons secrets, including navigation beams, to the British Embassy in Oslo. This leak became known as the Oslo Report.

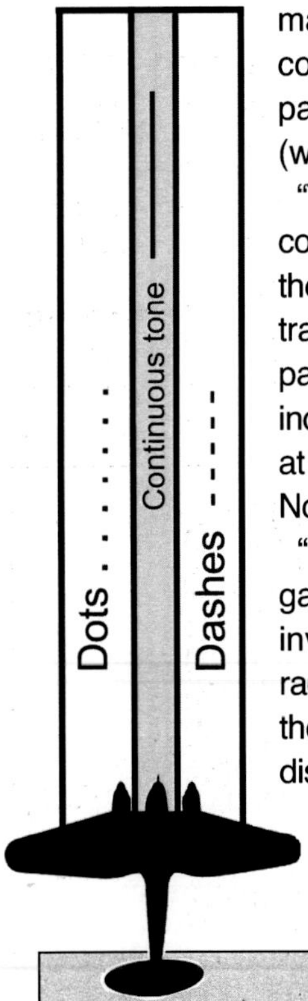

"In June 1940, Professor R V Jones, the eminent British scientist widely credited as the major player in German navigation beam countermeasures, was handed a piece of paper by the head of the RAF 'Y' Service (which intercepted German radio signals).

"The paper, which had been decoded by the code-breakers at Bletchley Park, mentioned the German word 'Knickebein', which roughly translates into English as 'Crooked Leg'. The paper also contained map coordinates that indicated the radio navigation beams were, at that time, crossing just south of Retford, in Nottinghamshire.

"Through scientific deduction, interrogation of captured enemy air crew and investigation flights, using aircraft fitted with radio receivers tuned to the frequency of the German radio beams, it was discovered that the beam system was based on existing pre-war equipment used by pilots to locate airfields and land in poor visibility and at night.

"The system consisted of a radio beam with Morse code type dots and dashes to either side, with a constant tone at the centre. The aircraft would fly along the centre of the beam – if it drifted off course the dots or dashes would guide the pilot as to which direction to steer the aircraft to get back on course. A second radio beam would intersect with the first over the target - the bombs would be dropped at that point

"Men were posted in structures at points across the country, described as tiny garden sheds (with floors), atop 300ft radio masts. They were equipped with a radio receiver to establish if the direction of the Nazi beams could be detected from the ground, as it could be done using aircraft. Once the direction of the beams was discovered it was possible to calculate which cities the Germans intended to attack that particular evening.

"The 'Knickebein' beams were given the code name 'headaches' by the British. The solution to the problem was aptly named 'aspirin' by the boffins.

"It was discovered that a piece of electrical equipment, used in hospitals to cauterise wounds, operated on a similar radio frequency to the Nazi beams. A Harley Street doctor with specialist knowledge of these devices was put in a military uniform and sent round the country to 'acquire' some of this equipment.

"It was quickly adapted and used in conjunction with modified electronic landing beams, from our own airfields, to interfere with the German beams.

"Opinions vary as to the effectiveness of this first attempt at jamming, but the Germans did start to use a second radio beam navigation system, known as X-Verfahren (X-System). This is the system that helped guide bombers to Sheffield in December 1940. "X-Verfahren differed from Knickebein in several ways.

Knickebein used a modified radio landing system fitted to most German aircraft whereas X-Verfahren was only fitted to the aircraft of special 'pathfinder' squadrons. Kampfgruppe 100 was the pathfinder squadron used in the Sheffield Blitz. Kampfgruppe 100 were based at the town of Vannes, in France, at this time.

"Kampfgruppe 100 usually arrived first and bombed the target. The next wave of German bombers aimed at the fires Kampfgruppe 100

Simplified illustration of a German bomber flying along a navigational radio beam had created. The second blitz raid on Sheffield on the night of 15th/16th December saw the first implementation of a changed Luftwaffe policy that saw Kampfgruppe 100 dropping incendiaries, rather than the usual high explosive bombs.

"Knickebein used two intersecting beams - X-Verfahren used at least four. Bombers would follow a main navigation beam, sited at Cherbourg during the Sheffield Blitz. Three side beams intersected with the main beam at set distances from the target.

"Fitted to the bombers of Kampfgruppe 100 were the airborne components of the X-Verfahren, known as X-Gerät. Central to this system was a clockwork motor powered clock named X-Uhr (X-Clock).

"When the first cross beam was intersected it alerted the crew to navigate accurately along the main beam. When the second cross beam was reached the operator would operate a switch which started a hand on the X-Uhr clock, similar to the hand of a stopwatch. At the third cross beam the switch was operated again; this stopped the first hand and started another hand of the clock. When the second hand met the first hand of the X-Uhr the bombs were automatically dropped. The purpose of the clock was to measure the speed of the aircraft accurately, so the bomb dropping position could be calculated precisely by the X-Gerät equipment.

"The detection of the beams and the countermeasures employed against them was performed by RAF No.80 (Signals) Wing based in Radlett, Hertfordshire. Information was collected as to the next Luftwaffe target(s). This information came from messages decoded by Bletchley Park from signals sent to the German beam operators, instructing them in what direction the beams should be pointed for the current targets. Alternatively, information about the beam directions could be gleaned from both airborne and ground based radio detection systems.

"It was from Radlett that the authorities in Sheffield would have been warned that an air raid was expected on the city. Various reports give the time of the warnings as about 5pm. The warnings were given in very vague terms, indicating that there 'may' be a raid that night. The Sheffield authorities would not have been told about beams overhead as this was top secret information, gained from Enigma decodes. The wartime government went to great lengths to disguise the fact that encrypted German signals had been decoded.

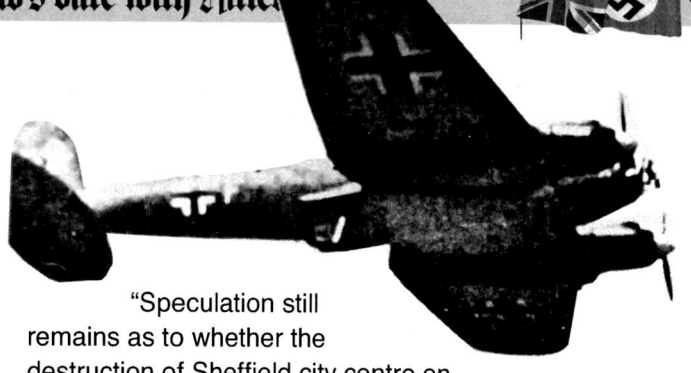

"Speculation still remains as to whether the destruction of Sheffield city centre on the night of 12th/13th December was a deliberate act, or a navigation error whilst trying to locate the factories of the east end (some records indicate that a portion of Kampfgruppe 100 did bomb visually). Other theories point to British scientists 'bending' the navigation beams to save the industrial parts of the city, leading to the city centre being decimated.

"'Ruffians' was the name given to X-Verfahren by the British scientists. Jamming of these beams was codenamed 'Bromide'; possibly this name was chosen as the object was to render the German beams impotent

"It has been noted by several authors and former Luftwaffe aircrew that X-Verfahren was not jammed or blocked effectively until mid January 1941, when 17 Bromide jammers were in operation throughout the country. At the time of the massive raid on Coventry, carried out a month before the Sheffield raids, the Bromide jammers are known to have been completely ineffective due to a calibration error by British technical staff.

Below left: German Knickebein radio navigation beam system

Below right: German X-Verfahren beam system

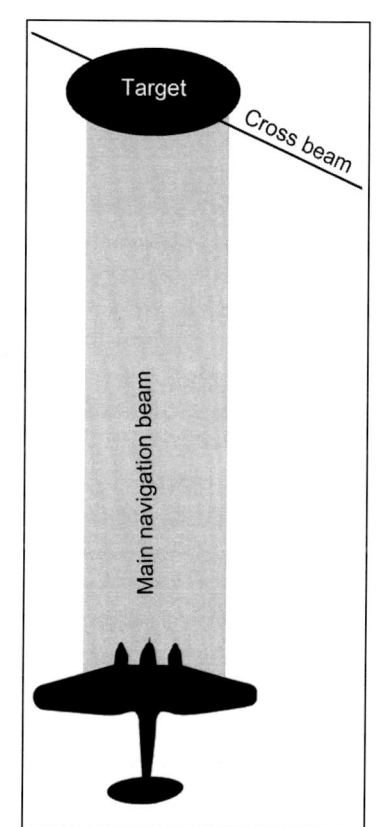

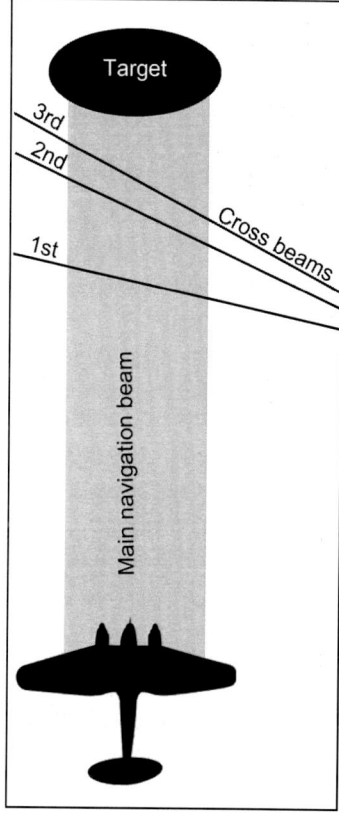

Sheffield's date with Hitler

"Professor RV Jones stated that 'In practice, there was not enough time to develop a synchronised system, so that all that we could hope for on most occasions was to confuse the German pilots and thus deprive them of the inherent accuracy of the beams; but as the battle went on the legend grew up on both sides that we were genuinely bending the beams'.

"It is said that Hitler used the phrase 'Coventrate' (after the devastating raid on Coventry in which the whole city was razed to the ground) to indicate total obliteration of British cities.

"Actual German bombing maps have also been discovered in the archives clearly marking Sheffield's hospitals, universities and museums, at the very heart of the city centre, as primary targets. Industrial targets in Sheffield's east end have been marked as secondary targets.

"At the time of writing it has just been announced that the Bletchley Park archive is to be scanned and made publically available via the internet. This archive may provide further clues to the Nazi's bombing intentions, such as the direction the beams were pointed on both nights of the Sheffield Blitz.

"If the beam headings for the first raid intersected over the city centre then Hitler's intentions would surely be quite obvious.

"If the beam headings crossed over the east end on both nights speculation will still remain as to the reason for the destruction of the city centre – navigation error or equipment failure? Or are there still secrets hidden in the archives showing that some form of beam-bending, accidental or intentional, did actually take place?"

Marples Hotel is a pile of rubble – left of picture

Salvaging household goods

Kathleen Wray was living at Cartmell Road in Woodseats at the time: "My mother was the type of person that befriended everybody and she took under her wing a younger lady whose husband was away in the forces. This lady was called Gladys Johnson and she had three young children aged four, two and a baby.

"Every time the sirens went we used to get up in the middle of the night, get dressed and rush round to Gladys Johnson's house so she wouldn't be by herself.

"On the morning of the Blitz this lady came knocking on our door and said 'if there's an air raid tonight don't come because Dennis', that was the eldest of her three kids, 'has got impetigo and I don't want your daughter to catch it'.

"So that night we didn't go and we spent the night on our cellar steps and Gladys Johnson, her three children and two lots of our neighbours were all killed in their shelter.

"It has always stayed with me that fate and impetigo saved our lives.

"I remember my mum taking me to town after the Blitz and seeing all the big shops like Walsh's and C&A that were down on the ground."

Memories of Redgates

Michael Nunn, former managing director of Redgates toy shop that was destroyed on the first night of the Sheffield Blitz, said: "My father was an air raid warden in Dronfield where we lived. There was nothing happening in Dronfield that night but I know my mother had converted one of the downstairs rooms into a sort of air raid shelter and my brother and I were shoved in there. My brother was five years younger than me. You could hear bumping going on and what not.

"I remember hearing the all clear go about 3 or 4 o' clock in the morning and my mother came in and said 'right you can go back to bed now'. My father was on an air raid post just around the corner. He came and took us outside and we could see the glow in the sky over the hills, Coal Aston and the hills between Dronfield and Sheffield. We couldn't see into Sheffield; we could see the red glow in the sky.

"And next day father set off to go into town as he used to every day. He was running the shop and he only got as far as Meadowhead. The police wouldn't let him go into town. He had to leave the car there and I think he walked into town from the top of Meadowhead and walked along London Road. He couldn't get up The Moor but got to the back of the old Redgates building and went round the corner and the whole place was in ruins.

"Apparently we used to have a firewatcher who used to live and stay in the premises overnight and my father always said he rang about 2 o' clock in the morning and the telephone was ringing but there was no reply obviously.

"This old bloke had buggered off. It turned out that the place was still OK then. But Woolworths next door was on fire and there was no water. The bombs had hit all the water mains and the fire brigade just couldn't do anything about it. That's my father's vivid memory.

"The offices were right in the middle; there was a safe there and father left the fireman pouring water in the safe to try and cool it down. They eventually got it open and all the previous day's takings were in there and they were all crumpled up and anyway, apparently, they took them to the bank and we got the money back!

"Father always tells me he was horribly upset. He walked up to the Grand Hotel which was in Leopold Street. They had a downstairs bar. It was a business man's pub. The sort of place where they all used to go at lunchtime and have a drink and so forth. Anyway father went and I think they had one or two! Jimmy Cockayne, who was the managing director of Cockaynes in Angel Street that was destroyed was there as well and there was one of the Roberts Brothers, who used to be on the Moor which was also hit. I think they all had a few drinks!"

Gladys Garfitt (who later became Gladys Everett) had her mother to thank for surviving the Blitz. She said: "I always wished I'd have told my mother that it was her that saved my life. We were ushered from the Elektra Cinema and told to go and shelter in The Marples Hotel but all I could think of was what my mother would think if she'd have found out I spent the night in a pub!

"We'd been watching a film called 'Green Hell' and we went out to a living hell.

"We sheltered at C&A Modes and that was hit. It was a miracle that I managed to crawl out of the rubble. Nobody made a fuss.

"We had to walk away from the flames with cars and trams on fire and windows were out everywhere. I remember all this jewellery hanging exposed from this jewellers' shop – nobody would have dreamt of taking it.

"We then went to this shelter with this little old lady who'd brought her budgie in a cage. We sat in there until the sirens went. I finally got to bed at 5am and was up again at 7am for work.

"What we saw walking through the Wicker was awful.

"My sister's friend was found nearly two months later. Where she had been buried had been so air tight her hair and nails had kept growing a long time after she died."

Rob Wainman's mother, Nora Gill, was another lucky Blitz survivor. She was working in the Boston Shoe Company in Attercliffe at the time of the attack. He said: "My mother was stood at the front door on a kind of runner of carpet and the blast from a bomb lifted her off her feet and totally pulled the carpet from under her."

Battle practice at Owlerton Stadium

72 **Sheffield's date with Hitler**

Blitz damage at Shiregreen

Rescue work at the Marples Hotel

CHAPTER NINE
Direct hit on the Marples Hotel

The Marples Hotel bombsite

The boisterous goings on at The Marples Hotel in Fitzalan Square in the city centre were typical of the Thursday night leisure activities going on across Sheffield on December 12, 1940 – the first night of the Sheffield Blitz.

Things were a world away from the entertainment industry that had virtually ground to a halt at the start of the war.

A ban had been imposed on people gathering in large numbers and cinemas, theatres and other entertainment centres were in darkness.

Sheffield magistrates announced places were closed 'until further notice' on September 5, 1939.

Dorothy Welsby: "That was the thing that hit me the most in the early days of the war. I couldn't believe our only light relief was being taken away from us. It seemed a bit extreme. My trip to the Sunbeam in Firvale was the highlight of my week."

The ban ended up lasting less than a fortnight. No bombs had dropped on Steel City and common sense prevailed.

Sheffield Lyceum reopened its doors on September 15 with Harry Hanson's Court Players staging 'French Without Tears'.

The projectors were soon cranked back into life at the scores of cinemas in the city after it was agreed an announcement would be made from the stage if an air raid was imminent.

Picture house managers were soon announcing record attendance figures.

"To hell with Hitler. I'm going to the pictures!" became the regular rallying cry.

The 'Keep Calm and Carry On' attitude of the Government's propaganda machine didn't ring more true than in Sheffield's licensed premises that night, just a few days before Christmas 1940, as thousands of locals put the thoughts of war aside and looked forward to Yuletide festivities.

Sheffield's date with Hitler

High Street looking towards Haymarket and Commercial Street after the Blitz, temporary C & A Modes store to the left, site of Marples Hotel, right, Yorkshire Penny Bank in background

They came from the four corners of the city to fill the cinemas, ballrooms and theatres of the city centre in a bid to get some relief from rationing, food shortages and loved ones being thousands of miles away fighting on the front line.

Snooker legend Joe Davis was typical of the attitude. The World Billiards Champion was all set to board a train from Hull to Sheffield to play an exhibition match at The Marples Hotel that night. It was only earlier bomb damage to the railway network that stopped him travelling – a fact that probably saved his life.

As it was, those who were still drinking didn't even have chance to put their glasses down as the venue received a direct hit, just a few minutes before midnight on December 12, 1940.

The imposing Marples Hotel was viewed as a pretty robust building.

Seven storeys high, it had its own concert hall, residential suites and grand lounge, as well as a number of bars and guest rooms and an extensive network of cellars.

Many people were caught unawares by the attack in the area and ignored the 7pm sirens thinking it was another false alarm.

You can only imagine the terror on their faces as incendiary bombs turned buildings in the vicinity of Fitzalan Square into raging infernos.

Many were left with little choice but to find shelter in The Marples Hotel. They were probably relieved to go inside and find the mood rather more upbeat. Customers and staff were calm and even singing popular tunes of the day whilst all hell was breaking loose outside.

The first sign of real danger – as far as the party goers inside were concerned – was the adjacent C&A Modes Ltd store taking a direct hit at 10.50pm.

Putting out the Blitz fires

Salvaging furniture after the Blitz

Sheffield's date with Hitler

The recently built premises of the flagship store were demolished in the blink of an eye.

The severity of the blast blew out the ground floor windows at The Marples Hotel with flying debris causing extensive damage to the building and injuring many people inside.

You can only imagine the panic and horror that went through the minds of the scores of people inside as the blast shock the very foundations of the building.

The one saving grace for the Sheffield city centre was the fact that the shops were empty at night and casualties would be fewer – however ferocious the raid.

The same wasn't to be said of the pubs, hotels and other entertainment venues.

In fact people had become that blasé to the air raid sirens that in cinemas at least, most people continued to watch the movie until it became perfectly clear that this was no false alarm.

The 400 people seated in Central Cinema on The Moor were left in no doubt – the roof caught fire.

All credit to them, they left in an orderly manner for the nearby shelters.

It was a repeat performance at all theatres and picture houses in the city centre – they all cleared in line with police orders.

The lack of widespread hysteria was played out across scores of venues – a factor that probably saved countless lives.

The majority of residents and customers in The Marples Hotel, unbeknown to them as they rushed to take cover in the basement, had less than an hour to worry about the situation after C&A Modes Ltd was flattened.

They doubtless thought they'd be safe as they huddled together in the subterranean depths of the cellars under Fitzalan Square. There were also soldiers in the building attending to the wounded and applying field dressings. And what were the odds of another direct hit just yards away from C&A Modes Ltd? Surely slight.

At 11.44pm on Thursday, December 12, 1940, The Marples Hotel took a direct hit.

Up to 70 people died. The exact number has never been known due to the inability to find and identify all the bodies as the seven storeys above collapsed like a pack of cards, leaving a scene of utter carnage.

Corporation Tram Inspector Richard William Reading was in the nearby tramways office in Fitzalan Square when the bomb hit.

He said: "When I got outside I saw that Marples Hotel had been hit. The building had collapsed and where it had stood there was a heap of rubble about 15 feet high.

"Things looked that bad the authorities didn't even consider looking for survivors until 10 hours later; a full 6 hours after the 4am all clear."

Bringing a survivor out of the rubble of the Marples Hotel

JACK TOMPKINS:
"I lived in Wallace Road. Our house got bombed and we were in the air raid shelter sited about 14 feet away. Our next door neighbour asked my mum if they could come into our shelter. She said 'yes'. We heard all this bombing. When the all clear sirens went we got out of the shelter and discovered our house had been bombed and was on fire like the others on the street. Our next door neighbour's shelter was blown up. It left a massive crater. I always said it was a landmine. My mother climbed into what was left of our house to see if she could find anything. She found a few boxing cups belonging to my dad who was wounded in Dunkirk."

MARION STEVENS:
"I was at the Empire with my mother hoping to see Henry Hall. But, much to my disappointment, we were asked to leave when the sirens went. We were taken to a building nearby which made cardboard cartons but, when it caught fire, we were moved elsewhere. As we sat and waited for the all clear, watching families from round the town coming in from their bombed houses, I kept saying to mum 'Won't there be a long queue for a tram to get home!' We walked to the Wicker Arches, climbing over rubble and debris, finally arriving at Shiregreen.

"The first thing my father said was 'Where have you two been all night?'

"I can't remember my mum's reply!"

But the search wasn't in vain, by one o'clock the following afternoon, seven men had been freed alive.

Two of the rescued walked straight out and were never seen again – their identities have never been verified.

Was it the shell-shock? Did they avoid the authorities and publicity on purpose? We'll probably never know.

Death must have been instant for the scores that died - crushed under tons of rubble as the cellar roofs gave way

Whatever it was, it was a miracle that anyone managed to walk away.

Rescuers had to remove around 1,000 tons of rubble to get to them and five others who were identified as: John Watson Kay, aged 46, of Boma Road, Stoke-on-Trent; Edward Riley, aged 36, of Ecclesall Road, Sheffield; Ebenezer Tall, aged 42, Clarissa Street, Shoreditch; William Wallace King, Arbett Parade, Bristol and Lionel George Ball, Knowle West, Bristol.

Death must have been instant for the scores that died – crushed under tons of debris as the cellar roofs gave way.

The cellars consisted of several chambers – each with their own roof.

One cellar survived, along with the seven men it somehow kept safe.

Joan Sykes: "I remember the Blitz. I was sat in the pantry with my grandfather. My mother was in town, my father was working. They used to go in Marples after the film every Thursday but this particular night they didn't, they went somewhere else."

The Marples Hotel site took weeks to excavate. The bodies of sixty four people were recovered, as well as the partial remains of six or seven others. The youngest listed victim was a 22-year-old woman.

The bombsite stood derelict for years and became a focal point for those wanting to remember those that lost their lives in the Sheffield Blitz.

Haydn Anderson said: "People would regularly lay flowers on the site – when it was turned into a temporary car park many people refused to use it as a mark of respect.

"Though a new Marples traded on the site from 1959 until 2002, many people felt a war grave had been desecrated and boycotted it – my parents wouldn't go near it."

The Marples was one of nine pubs totally destroyed that night. Others include The Westminster on High Street; The Royal Oak on King Street; The Devonshire Arms on South Street, The Moor; The Shades Vaults on Watson's Walk which dated back to 1797; The Three Horse Shoes on Norfolk Street; The Kings Head on Change Alley which dated back to 1772 – the whole of Change Alley was demolished in later years to make way for the construction of the modern day Arundel Gate; The Angel which sat on the corner of Angel Street and Bank Street which was even older having been in existence since 1657 and The Bodega on High Street [known prior to 1904 as The George].

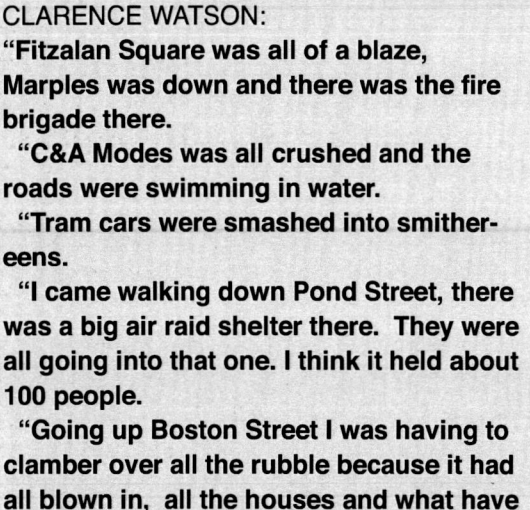

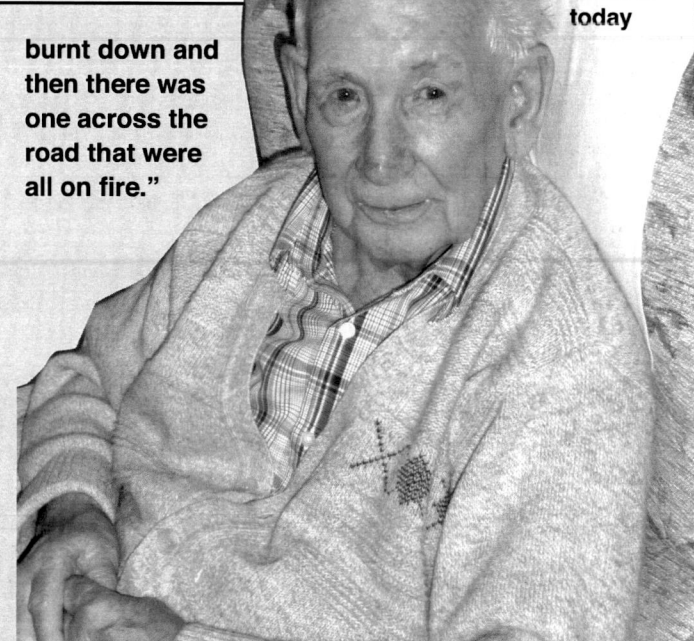

Clarence Watson as he is today

CLARENCE WATSON:
"Fitzalan Square was all of a blaze, Marples was down and there was the fire brigade there.

"C&A Modes was all crushed and the roads were swimming in water.

"Tram cars were smashed into smithereens.

"I came walking down Pond Street, there was a big air raid shelter there. They were all going into that one. I think it held about 100 people.

"Going up Boston Street I was having to clamber over all the rubble because it had all blown in, all the houses and what have you. All I could see were flames and when I got to the top, where the Locarno is, I could see the chip shop and that had been burnt down and then there was one across the road that were all on fire."

Instinct saved Winifred's life

Rachael Hope still holds a letter from her gran, Winifred May Stokes of Greenhill, where refusal to listen to a warden saved her life: "I was waiting to meet friends outside the Empire Theatre – Henry Hall and his band were topping the bill – when the guns started firing and incendiary bombs started falling.

"I thought I had better go home as quickly as possible – we lived at the bottom of Woodhead Road, so I ran from the Empire along Porter Street.

"People were making for the big air raid shelters in Porter Street, but I wanted to get home if possible as my mother would be frantic with worry.

"An ARP warden grabbed me by the arm and asked me where I was going. When I told him he said: 'You'll never make it love . Get yourself in here'.

"I found myself in a big shelter with many people in it. I was frightened, but I also had an urgent feeling to get out of that shelter. I can't explain it even now – premonition, perhaps?

"Anyway, in the general confusion of people coming into the shelter I slipped out and ran like hell.

"I got to the football ground and by this time bombing was worse, terrific explosions, shrapnel whizzing round and buildings falling around. I stood dazed and was suddenly grabbed and rushed into a shelter.

" I stayed there for the rest of the terrible hours and I knew a lot of people in that shelter.

"At last the all-clear sounded and we all emerged to a new world. I ran around the corner, and there was my house, thank God, still standing. Very battered about, but still there. My mum and dad were all right.

"But the shelter in Porter Street was hit that night with terrible loss of life. I can only thank God I got out of it."

Blitz survivor Winifred May Stokes

The clear up begins in Sheffield

Sheffield's date with Hitler

SIGHTSEERS, KEEP OFF BOMBED AREAS!
Vital Repair Work Must Not Be Hindered

KEEP AWAY FROM BOMBED AREAS if you have no business there—in other words there must be no sightseeing. This is by order of the Chief Constable of Sheffield (Major F. S. James), who states that people will hinder vital repair work if they do not carry out these instructions.

Major F. S. James told "The Star": "The progress has been splendid, the efforts of all services have been truly wonderful. Police assistance has come from the West Riding, Bradford, and Leeds, and every assistance has been offered by the military.

The conduct of the civilian population has been magnificent. They definitely have their chins up."

Appealing for motorists to give lifts, Major James said: "It is hoped that all motorists who have spare seats will give them available to those who have urgent business to attend."

FOLLOW THIS ADVICE

Here is official information and advice for all Sheffield people.

WATER

People in some districts must not use water from their taps for any purpose until properly notified. They must draw water from the mobile tanks.

DRINK WATER AND MILK ONLY THAT HAS BEEN BOILED.

FOOD

"The food position in Sheffield is satisfactory, although there may be temporary local difficulty over distribution," states Mr. H. W. Holmes, Assistant Divisional Food Officer.

The Ministry of Food are making supplies of rationed goods available to the shops throughout the city.

RATION BOOKS

Retailers are asked to supply rationed goods on demand to people who have no ration cards but they are also asked to take the precaution of ascertaining the names and addresses of the persons concerned in order to ensure that rationed goods are not obtained and taken outside the city.

A reminder is given of the serious penalties in regard to hoarding. Those people who have ration books should produce them.

The official also said that bread was to be issued under the Divisional Bread arrangements.

A considerable quantity of meat is to be provided for cooking-up so that cooked meals will be available for distribution to consumers.

A large quantity of margarine is coming into the city to aid local distribution. Any difficulties of local supply of commodities will be dealt with at once by the Ministry of Food.

The Food Office at present operating at the Licensing Department of the Town Hall.

INFORMATION

A central information bureau has been opened at the Central Library where people can obtain...

COAL

Sheffield people need have no worries about coal supplies. Coal depot managers had a special meeting yesterday under the House Coal Distribution Emergency Scheme, and arrangements were made so that no householder need be without coal.

"In achieving this object we want the co-operation of the public," said an official. "When people have supplies in hand they should not make immediate demands on their distributors. People without stocks will be supplied first and they should make immediate contact with the dealers with whom they are registered.

"Stocks are available in the depots and at the collieries."

All registered distributors should immediately contact their depot managers.

LETTERS

The public is asked by the Postmaster-Surveyor not to post letters in roads which the G.P.O. vans cannot reach, but he promises that if it is humanly possible to clear a letter box it will be cleared.

Letters should, if possible, be posted in boxes at the G.P.O. to convenient places for the G.P.O. to reach.

There will be two deliveries each day until further notice. The first in the morning at 9 a.m. and the second early in the afternoon.

SCHOOLS

Dr. W. P. Alexander, Sheffield Director of Education, told our reporter all school teachers were being mobilised to assist in dealing with homeless people.

The schools are closed until further notice.

* * *

Excessive noise may be heard which is likely to be associated with the demolition of property. Do not be alarmed.

* * *

Every effort is being made to renew normal transport services, and good progress has been made in this direction. On many train routes buses have been substituted.

* * *

Offers of clothing are being received by the authorities. Clothing should be sent to the Women's Voluntary Services in the Town Hall.

People who have not already registered their premises for billeting and are prepared to offer accommodation are asked to register at the Central Library.

SHEFFIELD'S MAGNIFICENT SPIRIT—SEE STORY ON PAGE 3.

Damage at Bramall Lane

Air raid damage looking up Fitzwilliam Street

CHAPTER TEN
December 25, 1940 -
the darkest Christmas in living memory

Christmas 1940 has got to go down as one of the bleakest in Sheffield's history.

The German blitzkrieg of a few days earlier had left hundreds dead; thousands homeless and much of the city's infrastructure destroyed.

Over 300,000 people were without water, 50 electricity sub stations were out of action and more than 3,000 telephone lines were damaged.

Much of the city centre lay in ruins along with home-grown department stores like Redgates, Walsh's, Cockaynes and Atkinsons. A total of 1,200 shops and business premises were totally destroyed.

War time censorship forbade full details of casualties and damage being published immediately. This led to widespread rumours of a death toll far higher than the actual one, later stated as over 660 with hundreds more injured.

The threat of a full scale German invasion was still a very real one.

Their forces were already within 25 miles of the English south coast in occupied France and much of Western Europe had already been overwhelmed by Hitler's blitzkrieg.

Bombing of Birmingham, Bristol, London, Manchester, Merseyside and Southampton had also taken place that month.

Christmas was actually one of the few traditions that survived in the war in some shape or form.

Guy Fawkes' Night was banned immediately as gunpowder production was needed for the war effort and bonfires contravened the blackout.

Sheffield Lord Mayor and Mayoress entertain members of the forces from convalescent homes in the city – note the beer warning on the wall above

Entertainment at a play centre for young victims of the Blitz

High Storrs Rest Centre

Sheffield's date with Hitler

Summer holidays became a thing of the past and Easter all but disappeared as chocolate – and real eggs – went 'on the ration'.

There was no ringing of church bells on Christmas day – they were banned, only to be rung as a signal that enemy forces were landing.

Christmas 1940 was the first one 'on the ration' for the citizens of Sheffield.

Weekly rations were 4oz bacon and/or ham; 6oz butter and/or margarine; 2 oz tea, 8 oz sugar and 2 oz cooking fats; meat, which was rationed by value, was reduced from 2s 2d to 1s 10d from December 16.

As a special treat, for the week prior to Christmas, the tea ration doubled to 4 oz and sugar increased from 8 to 12 oz.

Turkeys were available on the wholesale market but few shops were buying them because they were so expensive.

The fall of France meant French goods, like brandy, had almost disappeared from the shelves.

Dorothy Welsby said: "At this point it felt like nothing could stop Hitler. Many people were amazed we got to Christmas in 1940 with Britain surviving as a nation at all. The weather was grey and was so was the mood. It was an awful time but I remember my parents doing all they could to lighten the mood."

Many were told to stop using tap water for fear of disease breaking out through contamination. All water and milk had to be boiled before consumption.

Despite all this – Sheffielders did everything they could to celebrate

The city's High Storrs Rest Centre, for example, provided festivities for scores of children who survived the Blitz. Hundreds of Sheffield citizens celebrated Christmas in strange surroundings

The Blitz might have disrupted preparations for Sheffield's two Christmas pantomimes, Cinderella and Mother Goose, but it didn't stop them, despite some of the actors being bombed out of their lodgings and some rehearsals having to take place in Manchester.

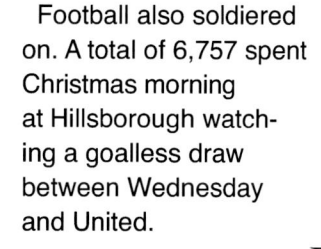

Football also soldiered on. A total of 6,757 spent Christmas morning at Hillsborough watching a goalless draw between Wednesday and United.

Above:
The King's Head, then the city's oldest hostelry, was a casualty of the Blitz – it first appeared in the Burgery Accounts in 1572

Below:
Campo Lane decimated

LORD MAYOR'S PARLOUR,
TOWN HALL, SHEFFIELD, 1.
DECEMBER, 1940.

TO THE PEOPLE OF SHEFFIELD

During the past days we have spent every available minute in visiting all parts of the City, and in helping to make arrangements to relieve the sufferings of those in distress; for we were convinced that this was a time for "Deeds not words."

But on this day, the Eve of Christmas, we are prompted to pause for a few moments and address this message to you all.

To those who have suffered bereavement, we express our deepest sympathy. May you find comfort in the knowledge that the thoughts of your fellow citizens are with you in your dire distress.

To the injured, will you allow us to wish you a speedy return to good health.

To those who have lost their homes and also those who have had to leave them, we sincerely trust that in their temporary accommodation they have found understanding friends. To those who, during the raid and since, have worked with untiring energy and gallantry, may we convey our warmest thanks. And to all Sheffield Citizens—may we express the hope that the spirit of Christmas will, in its noblest sense, inspire you with the tremendous courage needed to grapple successfully with the difficulties and trials that confront you.

Sheffield is still a City of proud and determined citizens! Sheffield is your City and ours.

We beg of you, then, to join with us in a firm resolve to carry on and to play our part until victory is achieved. Good-Luck and God Bless You.

Luther F. Milner
Lord Mayor.

Lottie Milner
Lady Mayoress.

Sheffield's date with Hitler

83

Making the best of Christmas 1940 – just days after the Sheffield Blitz

High Storrs Rest Centre

Business as usual after the Blitz

CHAPTER ELEVEN
The Blitz clear up and the Atkinsons story

Sheffield endured nine and a quarter hours of bombing on the December 12/13 and a further three hours on December 15/16.

Some parts of the city centre took two decades to recover.

Nearly 3,000 homes were totally demolished, 3,000 badly damaged and a further 72,000 with slight damage. There were 90 sewers broken and 206 water mains fractured.

On the roads there were 31 trams and 22 buses destroyed or severely damaged. Tram-wires were broken in 30 places and 857 street lamps were either destroyed or damaged.

Eight schools were razed to the ground with a further ten badly damaged; 18 churches were destroyed with many others damaged

Priority was given to feeding and finding accommodation for people who had lost their homes, clearing roads, getting public transport restarted and knocking down dangerous buildings in the days that followed.

Surrey Street's Central Library set up an information bureau to help residents with their post-Blitz problems.

Bombed-out shops and businesses made hasty arrangements to start up in alternative premises.

Defiance was in the air – everybody threw themselves behind the business of clearing up.

Scores of stories of bravery by rescue squads, nurses, fire fighters, ambulance drivers, police, air raid wardens and members of the public started to emerge.

Sheffield's behaviour in the Blitz was held as an example to all in a 1942 Ministry of Information booklet on the bombing of British cities.

Clearing up after the Sheffield Blitz

Sheffield's date with Hitler

Atkinsons after the Blitz (left of photo) looking up what's left of The Moor

Inset: Atkinsons advertising temporary offices in Millhouses within hours of the Blitz

Sheffield's longest standing family department store, Atkinsons, was probably more prepared than most city centre shops for an impending attack.

But it couldn't place the blame for the loss of virtually every single scrap of paperwork belonging to the retailer, including the details of tens of thousands of pounds owed to the store by thousands of customers, at the door of Adolf Hitler or head of the Luffwaffe, Goering. That was definitely down to human error on the part of an Atkinsons member of staff, they found out later.

There was no Sheffield department store more successful in the years leading up to the Second World War – the place absolutely thrived.

It was as much a part of the fabric of Steel City as the statue of Vulcan that perched proudly on top of the Town Hall and the "Made In Sheffield" tag that was synonymous with the standard of the artillery shells coming by the truck load from the city to supply the men on the front line of battle.

The firm was founded by John Atkinson who first arrived in the city in 1865.

After working in sales for a number of years the 26 year old, with little capital to his name, unveiled a new city centre business dealing in lace, ribbons and hosiery in 1872.

High quality service and value for money were at the core of his operation from day one – a business which was soon expanding into neighbouring shops and adding everything from furniture to clothing to its retail offering.

The burgeoning Atkinsons empire continued to grow at a phenomenal rate and by 1901 the foundation stone for its first, all-in-one store was being laid.

By 1922 the store had a staggering 46 departments and was decked out like never before to celebrate the store's Golden Jubilee.

It was the shopping trip of a lifetime for many at the time.

The decorated multi-level, atrium structure complete with glass roof was a site to behold for their celebratory year.

A full time horticultural expert looked after every conceivable floral arrangement which adorned the store. Live chickens and other livestock were housed on the ground floor, specifically to entertain the kids, whilst the resident pianist and regular classical quartet kept the adults in good spirits.

All in all it wasn't bad for a store that, only a few year earlier, had seen part of its operation requisitioned as a machine shop to produce war supplies in WW1.

It also circulated free wool to Sheffield women who volunteered to knit hats to fit inside the tin helmets of soldiers to make the unwieldy items more comfortable.

Though Sheffield escaped lightly in the Zeppelin air raids of WW1, Atkinsons was taking no chances second time round and decided to do whatever it took to ensure irreplaceable customer ledger books, invoices and other paperwork were kept safe.

Atkinsons invested a small fortune in the installation of its own bomb-proof vault built in the bowels of the resplendent store.

Time and luck – at that point at least – was on its side.

Sheffield's date with Hitler

The vault was completed just days before the first night of the Sheffield Blitz.

Atkinsons, like the rest of the shops in Sheffield city centre that cold winter's day on December 12, 1940, was decked out with glittering Christmas window displays as the hours to blackout closed in.

Dorothy Welsby said: "Atkinsons was always renowned for its glittering window displays and the build up to Christmas, 1940, was no different. I remember an amazing array of fur coats, toys and festive decorations. It was the kind of nice thing that helped you forget there was a war on. We were always grateful for small pieces of normality like that."

By the early hours of December 13, 1940, Hitler had totally destroyed everything Atkinsons had worked for over the past 68 years. Raid after raid had turned the store into a pile of smouldering rubble and twisted metal.

The only recognisable aspect of the store was the two pinnacles that still stood in defiance against the Nazi attack.

Staff were still confident that their impenetrable, underground vault had kept their irreplaceable customer records safe.

It was at that moment that Atkinsons realised luck – that had been on their side since the day they started out in business in 1873 – had finally run out.

The member of staff responsible for the new vault had forgotten to close the door on the fateful night and the entire contents went up in smoke...

Inside Atkinsons prior to its destruction

But fortunately the goodwill built up by the store over preceding decades, together with the unbroken spirit of the Sheffield people, allowed Atkinsons to be up and trading within days of the attack.

The store and its staff showed amazing resilience, tenacity and spirit in the way they dealt with the situation.

It would have been easy, in light of all customer records disappearing detailing the thousands that was owed on credit,

Atkinsons ended up moving part of its business onto Fargate following the destruction of its premises on The Moor in the Sheffield Blitz (below)

for Sheffielders to do the dirty and not pay what they owed – something that would have probably finished the store for good.

Amazingly, totally the opposite happened.

Graham Frith said: "Within three months of the end of the Sheffield Blitz, 80% of the money owed was paid back to us by customers, voluntarily."

Whilst that was going on, Harold and Walter Atkinson, sons of John, who'd inherited the operation from their father, were showing their outstanding skill at improvisation.

Within a few weeks they were open for business once again in temporary premises in St Judes Church and a school room on Milton Street. They'd got a kiosk outside the railway station and their various departments were appearing everywhere from Central Cinema on The Moor to The Star and Telegraph building.

Silk from heaven in Crookesmoor Road

Dave Manvell:

"During the Sheffield Blitz, a landmine was dropped attached to a parachute, landing on Crookesmoor Road, close to Conduit Road.

"The whole area had to be evacuated for a few days, as the bomb disposal team was sent to disarm it. My father, who was home on leave at the time, was a member of the local ARP group and he watched as a very young man sat on the bomb and removed the fuse.

"After the bomb had been made safe, the parachute on which the bomb had come down was given to my father. Parachute silk was like manna from heaven and so my mum cut it up and gave it to local families, from which dresses and other items of clothing were made."

They even bought Tuckwoods high class grocers, that stood on Fargate, which they turned into a department store with restaurant.

It was a story played out across Sheffield as blitzed city centre stores like Cockaynes, Walshs, C&A Modes, Redgates and scores of others started on the road to recovery.

Atkinsons site on The Moor remained as a bombsite for the next two decades with only window facades giving an indication of what it used to be.

Their new store – the one that stands today – was finally opened in 1960.

— Our minds look back to twelve months ago.

A message of thanks - on the Eve of Christmas

"Be not affected by the temporary shift of fortune's winds. Be certain that your undertakings are based on the solid rock of proven worth. In a world of change, cling to that which endures."

We thank the many hundreds of customers and staunch friends who have given us the greatest possible help since a year ago; for their patience under every inconvenience, and their generous support through thick and thin.

We thank the big-hearted firms who have made their premises available to us, so that we could rise from our ashes, particularly—
The Sheffield & District Gas Company,
Sheffield Newspapers Ltd.,
The Central Picture House.

We thank the various Commercial Bodies and Trade Associations who have so magnificently lent us every aid.

We thank the Sheffield Corporation for their unfailing help and understanding.

We thank our many suppliers, in all parts of the Country, whose ready co-operation has enabled us to provide our customers with their needs, to repair their losses, and to offer them a large and varied choice.

Last, but not least, we thank our Maker for giving us the strength to cope with unprecedented difficulties.

JOHN ATKINSON Ltd
LEOPOLD ST. — HIGH ST. — THE MOOR

Refreshments outside Sheffield Town Hall

From bombsite to city centre oasis

There is story after story of bombsites inadvertently turning into exciting adventure playgrounds for kids across the city.

It came as no surprise.

But one small corner of the the city centre – instead of being left as a pile of rubble for years - took on a whole different and attractive guise and ended up growing and selling something that spelled the hopes and prayers of a whole nation after two horrific world wars – a symbol of peace that went on to replace the site where their Anderson Shelter had been months before for many.

This particular oasis of calm and hope for the future of Sheffield was all thanks to local landscape gardener Clifford Proctor.

The temporary rock garden on High Street

Haydn Anderson: "Bomb sites were quite the norm for kids like us growing up in the East End of Sheffield during WW2. As youngsters, we didn't appreciate the full horror of what they signified. We just looked on with interest at the devastation.

"It was strange to be able to see bedroom wallpaper and a fireplace, high up on the only remaining wall of a house. Suddenly what had been private was brutally exposed.

"After the damaged properties were dismantled and cleared to make them safe, they served as very interesting play areas, as there was always lots of rubble left around to investigate. I well remember looking on in amazement as potatoes sprouted up on the bomb site near my grandmother's house on Birch Road, Attercliffe. We didn't realise they would have been part of the previous occupants vegetable store.

"When the war ended, rebuilding the badly damaged parts of the city centre began, and slowly the advertising hoardings that had hidden the bomb sites were taken down and foundations laid for new exciting modern buildings. This all took time of course – the iconic Sheffield store, Walsh's, opened their new premises in 1953.

"A less documented temporary development took place around 1950, opposite Kemsley House, at the corner of High Street and George Street. There, right in the middle of the tired city centre, on a flattened site, a little oasis emerged. It was a garden, courtesy of the Chesterfield horticultural firm of Clifford Proctor.

"Beautifully laid out with roses, exotic border plants, shrubs and small trees, it was a real tonic, and not only that, you could order plants from the little wooden sales office at the back.

"They had a wonderful display of roses, with established varieties like 'Ena Harkness', 'Crimson Glory' and 'Spek's Yellow', but the star rose of the moment was a new variety, developed in France, and aptly named 'Peace'.

"I remember we symbolically planted them on the site of our Anderson Shelter.

"Where we lived, a decent privet hedge provided the greenery (golden privet if you were a bit grander) and Nasturtiums gave a splash of colour. If you were keen, dahlias and chrysanthemums were grown.

"Taking an interest in gardening at this time, I was spellbound by the range of exotic sounding plants on offer, most of which I had never heard of, and determined to bring a little bit of this magic to our back garden in Attercliffe. Consequently, the feathery plumes of astilbes, towering delphiniums and the like, started to appear in the East End all thanks to Proctors."

Haydn Anderson in the war years

Haydn Anderson today

> **NELLIE BENNETT:**
> "Six months after the Blitz they dug a body out on Ellesmere Road. It was a soldier and he had been sheltering in the passageway."

SHEFFIELD SCHOOL CARING FOR 500 HOMELESS

"God knows what we should have done without a place like this to come to," was the heartfelt tribute of a Sheffield woman, who has lost her home and belongings, to the efforts of the staff of the High Storrs Grammar School who have fed and housed over 500 people since Friday morning.

"THEY have all been wonderful," said Mrs. Howard, who was sharing a schoolroom with a family of eight from Pitsmoor. "They have given us hot food, found us somewhere to sleep and even looked after the children for us."

Behind these expressions of remarkable story of high peed improvisation and unselfishness by the teachers of the Grammar School and the neighbourhood.

"Our school was never on the list of centres," Mr. Luther Smith, the headmaster, told a reporter of "The Star," but when we realised that every building capable of housing a number of people would be wanted we all volunteered to look after as many homeless as could be accommodated, and there has been a steady stream of people ever since Friday morning."

"My staff, men and women, have had hardly any sleep since the first raid, but they refuse to stop working.

"Even the boys and girls are helping as messengers, and in other capacities.

"The women teachers took over the feeding and sleeping arrangements, and have done wonders.

No praise can be too high for them.

"For the first three days we provided all the food and clothing ourselves, with the help of people in the district and Mr. Fretwell Downing, of Rustlings Road, who has not only found food, but cooked it as well."

PRAMS PROVIDED

For the first three days people in the neighbourhood swarmed to the school, bringing parcels of food, clothing, and toys. Some even provided prams for babies.

Mr. Downing did the cooking, and no one at High Storrs has been without at least two hot meals a day.

To-day he went to Fir Vale and collected 11cwt. of sausages, hundreds of pieces of filleted fish, and sacks of potatoes.

Some of it is being cooked on the spot by Army cooks, who have been sent up for that purpose. Mr. Downing cooked the rest in his bakery ovens.

Some of the women and children needed medical attention and two sick bays were arranged so that these could be dealt with at once.

A local doctor, Dr. E. Rosenfield, volunteered his services, examined all the cases and saw to it that where necessary they were removed.

TAKEN FOR WALKS

Mrs. S. A. Wilde, a member of the W.V.S., who originally went to the school to help with the feeding arrangements, transferred herself to the sick bays, and also arranged for those people who had to be removed to be taken to the Church Hall at Dore.

Nothing was forgotten. The women teachers even took parties of the children out on to the playing fields to see that they got some fresh air and exercise.

Some of the adults are helping wherever they can inside the school. One man was sweeping a corridor, another helping to carry water. Others were going into town to make inquiries about relatives or sending messages to soldier fathers.

One young married woman, Mrs. E. Welton, who escaped from a blazing house with her four young children, was particularly anxious that her husband, stationed with the "Koylis," should know that his wife and children were all right.

Mrs. Welton got out of a side door which was fortunately open, pulled the pram out, and packed her four children, Dorothy and Brenda, four month-old twins, Pauline, 16 months old, and Maureen, three years old, on to it.

Then she rushed them all up to High Storrs where she has been ever since Friday afternoon. She could not speak too highly of all that had been done for them.

MIRACLE OF SPEED

In another room were Mr. and Mrs. Gill with five children of their own and a daughter-in-law with a baby. They all escaped when their street was hit by a bomb, and had just finished a hot breakfast when our reporter spoke to them.

"The teachers here are ladies and gentlemen," said Mrs. Gill. "They've done wonders for us."

In every other room similar tributes were paid. The organisation has been a miracle of speed and enterprise.

A prominent figure among the staff helpers is Mr. J. R. Wassell, who refused to stop working although his right arm is in bandages.

NARROW ESCAPE

Mr Wassell was with the rescue party in which Mr. T. Parramore, of Ringinglow Road, lost his life, when a bomb struck a house in which they were rescuing a trapped soldier. "Some woodwork formed a triangle over me," said Mr. Wassell, "otherwise I would have been killed, too. I was lucky to get out with nothing worse than a lacerated arm. Anyhow, we got the soldier out whom Mr. Parramore was trying to save and he is alive."

Billeting officers are gradually transferring people from High Storrs Grammar School to private homes, but as long as there are homeless to look after the work will go on there. And great work it is.

* * See also Pages 5 and 6.

HITLER'S WAR
472nd Day.

BLACK-OUT & LIGHTING-UP TIMES:
5.17 p.m. to 8.40 a.m. to-morrow.

Moon rises to-night at 1.1 p.m. and sets to-morrow at 10.57 a.m.

Marks & Spencer found a temporary home in the building that became better known as the Locarno, on London Road, after its store was destroyed in the Sheffield Blitz. It is now Sainsburys.

CHAPTER TWELVE
VE Day - peace finally returns to the streets of Sheffield

VE Day celebrations on Upper Valley Road in Meersbrook

92 — Sheffield's date with Hitler

Burtons and C&A Modes in the late 1930s prior to the bombing that destroyed them both

Right: The attitude that became a role model for other UK cities facing air attack is plain to see in this graphic that appeared in The Star just hours after the Sheffield Blitz

DEFIANT!

VE celebrations in Rushdale Avenue

Sheffield's date with Hitler

VE Day (Victory In Europe Day) came on May 8, 1945. Britain had been at war for nearly six years. This was the day the Allies accepted the unconditional surrender of the armed forces of Nazi Germany and the Third Reich. Adolf Hitler had shot himself just days earlier in his Berlin bunker.

The sacrifices of Sheffield and the country had not been in vain.

The Blitz might have destroyed much of the physical heart of the city but it didn't break its spirit. If anything it made more resilient.

The steelworks went on working throughout the war, much of them operated by the women of the city whilst the men fought at the frontline.

Seventy years since the Sheffield Blitz and it's hard to imagine the horrors and sacrifices endured by the people of the city on the two nights in December 1940 and through the whole six years of war.

It was their spirit – and the spirit of counterparts in other bombed cities like Birmingham, Liverpool, Bristol, Southampton, Plymouth, Coventry and London – that helped carry the country to victory.

The war in the Far East continued until August 14, 1945, when the Japanese surrendered and WW2, the most devastating conflict in the history of mankind, was finally over.

VJ celebrations on Carlton Street

The "Big Three" allied leaders (seated) Winston Churchill, Franklin Roosevelt and Joseph Stalin at the Yalta summit in 1945 to discuss Europe's post war reorganisation after the fall of Hitler

94 Sheffield's date with Hitler

The big campaign of 1944 encouraged Sheffielders to holiday at home – here they are dancing in the open air to wind-up gramophone records

Ecstatic smiles on VE Day

Sheffield's date with Hitler

95

The aftermath of the Sheffield Blitz looking across Devonshire Green

VE Day celebrations outside Sheffield Town Hall

Sheffield's date with Hitler

Crowds gather to hear Sheffield's Thanksgiving week funds have reached £500,000 in September 1945

CHAPTER THIRTEEN
What's to see of the Blitz in the 21st century

People regularly complain about the faceless nature of many of the buildings in modern day Sheffield city centre.

The blame for this can be laid firmly at the feet of Adolf Hitler.

It was his Luftwaffe that decimated it and robbed Sheffield city centre of some of its grandest and most historic buildings on The Moor, High Street and other keys areas.

If you want to get a true appreciation of what Sheffield was like before those two devastating nights in December 1940, just stand outside the front entrance to Sheffield Town Hall and look to your right along Leopold Street, down Fargate.

The whole area survived with barely a scratch.

Look up at the buildings and you'll see, in the majority of instances, little has changed and you're largely seeing the same view the men enjoyed as they rushed to enrol for the Sheffield City Battalion in WW1.

It was his Luftwaffe that decimated it and robbed Sheffield city centre of some of its grandest and most historic buildings

Many bomb sites, following the Sheffield Blitz in WW2, lay derelict for years.

Bland concrete was the acceptable norm in the late fifties and sixties when many of the buildings were replaced – hence the situation today.

If you want to find out more about the lost buildings you should start with the Local Studies section of the Central Library on Surrey Street (which thankfully survived the Sheffield Blitz) which holds scores of pictures of Sheffield city centre before the bombing.

Top left: What was left of The Moor looking up towards Moorhead and Pinstone Street ater the Blitz

Top right: Looking the same way up The Moor today. The large store on the immediate left is Atkinsons which reopened in the early 1960s. Note the similar style of the buildings that replaced the whole Moor area that was decimated in the Blitz.

Sheffield's date with Hitler

Westbourne Road near the Botanical Gardens

Westbourne Road as it is today. There's no clearer sign of Blitz damage in the Sheffield suburbs than a couple of modern houses standing in the middle of a row of towering Victorian houses

Sheffield's date with Hitler

99

Blitz damage to Hillsborough's Hawksley Avenue. The row in the foreground of the picture was completely destroyed and subsequently rebuilt. The shock wave from the blast tore through the other side of the street but the houses were repaired. Below: Hawksley Avenue as it is today.

Top: Bomb damage on Cemetery Road and (above) the church as it is today.

Above: Bomb damage and its unsightly repair is clearly visible under the Wicker Arches and (right) Sheffield City Hall pillars are still riddled with shrapnel scars

Archibald Road in Nether Edge after the Blitz

Archibald Road as it is today. Like for like building has pretty much eradicated any sign of Blitz damage

Phoney War 1939

Feet and legs first descending wooden steps,
Tall Syd soon sitting in shelter's plain frame.
Heavy eyed terrified, white as a sheet,
Face lit up by flickering flame.

"Come in luv," muttered mum, stifling a tear,
"You'll be safe in here, until the all clear."
Dad, Cliff were on board last trams to get through.
We'll put the board back, the best thing to do.

The sight of the night, disappeared from view
We began to nod off: it didn't take long.
Exhausted Syd sleeping sleep of the dead
His confused wild story, ringing round in his head.

He'd walked home from the Wicker, via the Moor
A bright moon-light night inviting his tour.
Ack. Ack. started blazing, haphazard their aim
Peppering Sheffield roofs with ra - ta - tat rain.

Shrapnel's hail, beating down from the sky,
He dodged into passages, doorways near by
Saw houses burning, incend'ries on roofs
Exploding bombs told of all hell let loose.

During a lull, in that hellish night's fury,
A toff came along, holding a cane.
Tipped his bowler to Syd, asked most politely,
"Please help me one of these fires to restrain?"

Syd obeyed at once. Too astonished to argue.
Picked up the ends of a sandbag in haste
Two carried it to, the heat in the street,
Dropped it on top, with no time to waste.

Bizarre events were ten a penny that night.
One man, spending one, received such a fright.
When he pulled the chain, as needs he must,
Was suddenly covered; in plaster and dust!

Syd had survived the violent Luftwaffe's storm,
Later, we discovered his overcoat torn,
Shoulder to armpit, a jagged edged tear,
Though clothes rationed, no great loss to bear.

The Sheffield Blitz. Syd's story

A single word, black, on yellow, print paper
Three letters creased in tight wired claw.
Stark staring message, fear and bewilderment
Boy in short trousers viewing ominous war.

His dad - a terrier - a strange dog of conflict
Had fought on the Somme in nineteen sixteen
Traumatised, yet survived told "Pick up a rifle"
Too sick to respond - a sorry has-been.

His brothers, thirteen and sixteen, were bigger and stronger-
Years distant from him in more ways than one,
Interest in girls and clandestine smoking
Uniform attraction made civvy life dull.

I see it still, when nudged by history
A watershed a change, a line in the sand.
The flimsy paper, the dread word to mum
A tear in her eye when day's work was done.

The eleventh hour struck on that fate filled Sunday
Ended discussion, sharpened swords for the fight.
Mr. Chamberlain spoke from his heart to the nation.
Mr. Hitler spoke with the voice of armed might.

Early on an air raid, sounded the sirens
We sat in the shelter, gas masks on our knees.
Listening for wardens rattling their rattles
To don them in haste, have safe air to breathe. . .

Comedians sang about, hanging their washing out
On the Siegfreid Line. What a strange thing to do?
Dad went to work. We three lads went to school.
Mum slaved at home, little time of her own.

Woolworth's prices remained thre' pence and six pence
Across the street from the thirty bob shop,
But life was different; even I could sense it.
Everyone waiting, for that first bomb to drop.

This queer time later, was called Phoney War.
An unreal, bogus, fake feel hung about it.
In 1940 the sleep walking was over
Fully awake, all pitched in the thick of it.

by Roy Bellamy

Sheffield's date with Hitler

101

An aerial photograph of Sheffield immediatley after the Blitz

102 — Sheffield's date with Hitler

THE SHOPAHOLICS GUIDE TO 1970s SHEFFIELD

Pauldens • Walshs • Redgates • Cockaynes • Schofields • Sexy Rexy

By Neil Anderson

Starring all the old favourites... and more

DiRTY STOP OUT'S GUIDE to 1970s SHEFFIELD

By Neil Anderson

Starring:
- CLUB FIESTA
- CRAZY DAIZY
- PENNY FARTHING
- HOFBRAUHAUS
- BUCCANEER
- JOSEPHINE'S
- PENTHOUSE
- TOP RANK

and many more!

☆ The Star

THE REEL MONTY

Now with SHEFFIELD INTERNATIONAL CITY the follow up!

☆ The Star / Creativesheffield

City On The Move 35th anniversary edition

TINSLEY TOWERS

COLLECTORS' EDITION

520 PIECES JIGSAW APPROX. 50CM X 38CM

WWW.ACMRETRO.COM

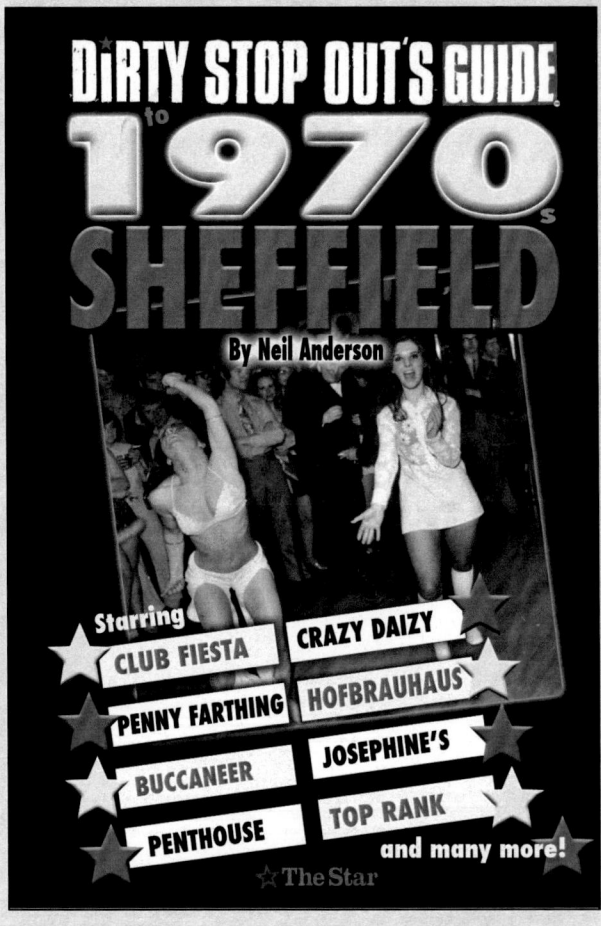

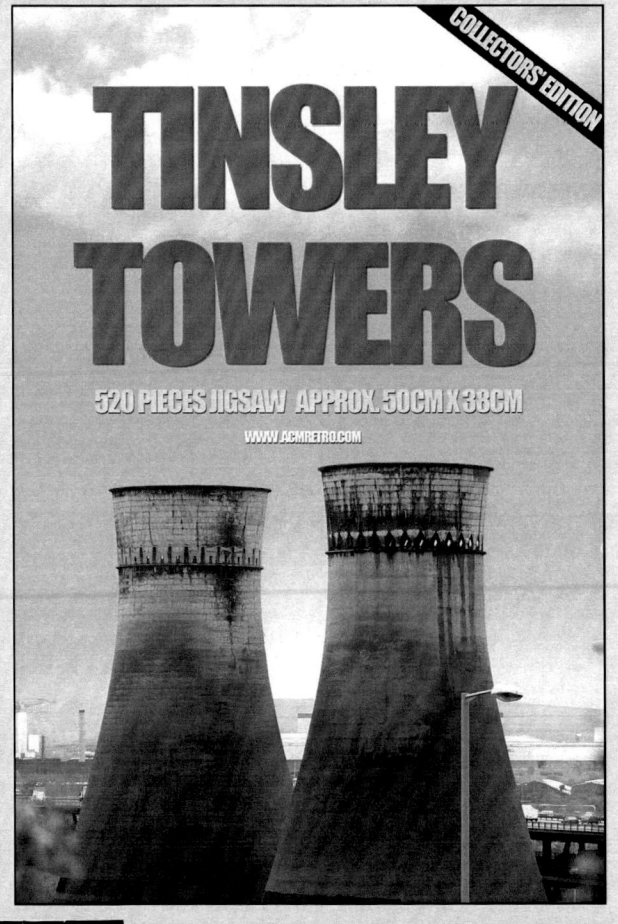

Also available from ☆ACM ЯETRO   www.acmretro.com

The Author

Neil Anderson's interest in Sheffield's involvement in both world wars started with childhood memories of time spent with his great grandad, Harold Hickson.

He was one of the first people to answer Kitchener's call and sign up for the Sheffield City Battalion in World War One.

The fighting force were part of one of the biggest military disasters in history – the Battle of the Somme in 1916. Harold was one of just a handful of survivors that came back to Sheffield and could only look on in horror as the country counted down to war once again in 1939.

His daughter, Neil's grandma, Dorothy Welsby, provided much first hand evidence of life in the Anderson Shelter before she died, aged 93, in September 2009.

Neil has written for titles spanning The Independent to the Yorkshire Post and was a Sheffield Telegraph columnist for over a decade.

Last year he wrote the best selling 'Take It To The Limit' book about the legendary West Street venue that opened in 1978 and followed up that with the 'Shopaholics Guide to 1970s Sheffield'.

His 'Dirty Stop Out's Guide to 1970s Sheffield' was published in June, 2010.

When he's not writing books he's busy running a successful media relations company (www.allcreditmedia.com).

Acknowledgements

Sheffield Newspapers for use of pictures and quotes, Sheffield Archives, Sheffield Local Studies Library for use of pictures and documents, Chris Hobbs, Imperial War Museum for use of pictures and posters, American National Archive, Graham Frith and Atkinsons, Michael Nunn and Redgates, Broomgrove Nursing Home staff and residents, Audrey Eaton, Haydn Anderson, Patricia Eales, Alan Wilson, Clarence Watson, Rachael Hope, Sandra Barley, Jane Salt, Paul Licence, Dave Manvell, Jack Tompkins, Joan Lee, Alice May Parkin, Gladys Everett, Kathleen Wray, Rob Wainman, Nora Gill and Michael Glover

Dedicated to the memories of Harold Hickson and Dorothy Welsby and the thousands of Sheffielders who lost their lives in WW1 and WW2.

Research, words, photography, proofing and balancing the books: Ian Cheetham
Book design and layout: Afb Creatives
Mail order: Karen Davies

All round inspiration: Lowri and Ewan Anderson
Inspiration, proofing and transcriptions beyond the call of duty: Lindsay McLaren

Bibliography

Abstract -Some historical and technical aspects of radio navigation in Germany over the period 1907 to 1945 by Arthur O Bauer

Beam Benders, No. 80 (Signals) Wing, 1940 – 1945 by Laurie Brettingham - Midland Publishing Ltd

Bomber Units of the Luftwaffe 1933 - 1945 Vol 2 by Henry L de Zeng IV & Douglas G Stankey - Ian Allan Publishing

Codebreakers - The Inside Story of Bletchley Park by F.H. Hinsley & Alan Stripp - Oxford University Press

Curious Tales of Yorkshire & Derbyshire by Dave Manvell with Annette Manvell - ALD

Enigma - The Battle for the Code by Hugh Sebag - Montefiore: Weidenfeld & Nicolson

First Blitz by Neil Hanson - Doubleday

Hitler by Ian Kershaw – Hutchinson of London

Instruments of Darkness - The History of Electronic Warfare, 1939 – 1945 by Alfred Price - Greenhill Books

It's a Bit Lively Outside by Joyce Holliday – Yorkshire Art Circus

Most Secret War - British Scientific Intelligence 1939 – 1945 by RV Jones - Hamish Hamilton

Raiders Over Sheffield by Mary Walton and J. P. Lamb – Sheffield City Libraries

Sheffield At War by Clive Hardy – Archive Publications

Sheffield Blitz by Paul Licence – A Star publication

Sheffield City Battalion by Ralph Gibson and Paul Oldfield – Pen & Sword

Sheffield In The 1930s by Peter Harvey – Sheaf Publishing Ltd

Sheffield Since 1900 by Peter Harvey – Archive Publications

The Blitz - Then and Now Vol 2 edited by Winston G Ramsey - Battle of Britain Prints International Ltd

The First Pathfinders - The Operational History of Kampfgruppe 100, 1939 – 1941 by Kenneth Wakefield - Crecy Books Ltd, 1992

The Luftwaffe War Diaries by Cajus Bekker – Macdonald & Co

The Radar War - Germany's Pioneering Achievement 1904 – 1945 by David Pritchard - Patrick Stephens Ltd

The Second World War Vol 2 by Winston S Churchill - Cassell & Co

Waves, Enigma and the Coventry Myth - British intelligence in WW II by Bob Thomas

Soldiers' widows, wives, old age pensioners and the unemployed receiving seeds and tools under the Sheffield Allotments for the Unemployed Scheme